The NAME GAME

The NAME GAME

The Decision that Lasts a Lifetime

Albert Mehrabian

Library of Congress Cataloging-in-Publication Data

Mehrabian, Albert.
The name game: the decision that lasts a lifetime
by Albert Mehrabian
160 p., 15 cm. x 23 cm.
ISBN 0-915765-75-6
1. Names, Personal--United States--Psychological aspects.
I. Title.
1. Consumer education--United States.
CS2367.M44 1990
929.4'0973--dc20
90-13470
CIP

PRINTED IN THE UNITED STATES OF AMERICA
First Edition

Acknowledgments

I owe a special debt of gratitude to Patricia Valdez, who worked with me during the initial phases of this project and helped gather a significant portion of the data reported here. I am also very grateful to several of my other students, including Linda Amann, Ellen Lin, Jeff Long, Marlina Piercy, Marily Simpson and Steven Whalen, who all contributed many long hours to collect the extensive survey data reported in this book.

Table of Contents

Preface

The *Name Game* was written to minimize intuition and guesswork, mistakes, and sometimes errors of tragic proportions in the naming process. First, it is addressed to parents-to-be and provides them with a systematic and intelligent approach to select names for their newborn. Also this book can help those who feel they have been given inappropriate, bothersome, or even handicapping names and who desire an objective and rational approach to selecting new names.

Readers who wish to skip preliminaries can refer to chapter three (where use of the tables is explained) and then proceed to the tables they need.

As part of my effort to continuously improve and refine the ratings in this book, I would appreciate feedback from those who use my name selection process. Let me know if there are names you would like included in our future surveys. More importantly, write me about your experiences with this name selection process. I would like to know about reactions from friends and relatives to the names you selected based on my method and the longer-term effects of the new names you select in this way.

Correspondence regarding your reactions will be invaluable in improving future editions of this book and can be addressed to me at P.O. Box 2568, Monterey, CA 93942-2568.

Albert Mehrabian
Monterey, CA

Chapter One

Selecting a Baby's Name

First impressions leave lasting impressions, especially in the age of fifteen-second commercials. Two factors create this first impression: your appearance and your name. We spend countless hours fine-tuning our appearance, buying the right clothing, getting our hair done, selecting eye glasses, or contact lenses. On the other hand, often very little thought or research goes into the choice of our names. Many names are selected on the basis of a whim, instinct or family tradition. You owe it to your children to select a name that will help them get through life and not handicap them.

We all tend to be aware of our physical characteristics and features. Our appearance delivers powerful messages about ourselves: a three-piece suit means one thing and a short skirt another. We alter our physical appearance and impressions by clothing, jewelry, hair styles, cosmetics and even surgery. We are acutely aware of the impact physical appearance can have on social and business relationships.

It is probably an understatement to say that most people have had occasion to wish they looked different, were taller, shorter, weighed less, had a trimmer body, had different natural hair coloring, or a smaller nose. In fact, the drastic extreme of plastic surgery is not uncommon as a way of modifying physical appearance. Every day, people use hair coloring, hair transplants and wigs to alter their appearance.

Our names, as well as our physical appearances, have a significant impact on how others react to us in social relationships and at work. Names give an impression before you meet others, on the telephone or in letters. The name we sign to a letter, a piece of art, or piece of writing contributes to the overall impression that letter or work makes on others. The name we mention to a stranger over the phone tells the stranger something about ourselves. Whether we are physically present or not, our names alter the impression we make.

Individuals in acting, politics, literature and the arts tend to be particularly name conscious. They sometimes assume new and more "exotic" names which, at least in terms of their intuitions, seem to be more suited to the images they wish to project to their audiences. The following chart lists prominent authors, actors and others who have changed their name:

Given Name	Adopted Name
Samuel Clemens	Mark Twain
Leslie R. King	Gerald Ford
Norma Jean Mortenson	Marilyn Monroe
Marion Morrisson	John Wayne
Israel Baline	Irving Berlin
Doris von Kappelhoff	Doris Day
Allen Kongisberg	Woody Allan
Archibald Leach	Cary Grant
Roy Harold Scherer, Jr.	Rock Hudson
Madonna Ciccone	Madonna
Prince Roger Nelson	Prince
Gary Hartpence	Gary Hart
Gordon Summers	Sting
Richard Starkey	Ringo

Company Names

Those who are involved with marketing a product or service are well aware of the importance of names. Many companies spend large sums to select effective product or service names and major corporations spend millions of dollars to devise a new corporate identity with a new name as the focal point. In 1972 Esso changed its named to Exxon at a cost of more than $100 million, the most expensive name change in history. Thousands of new gasoline station signs had to be erected around the country, and an extensive advertising campaign promoted the new name. When Sperry Rand merged with Burroughs in 1986 they spent millions of dollars to come up with a new name (Unisys).

Ordinary mothers and fathers do not have the resources to hire image consultants to help name their children. Think of the *Name Game* as your image consultant to help your child start off with a name designed to help him or her advance through school, college and work.

Psychological Effects

Parents-to-be need to consider that a child's name becomes part of the child's self image. Your name, like your physical appearance and personality, can play an important role in social and work relationships. Parents who invest untold hours toward the social, emotional and educational development of their children cannot afford to be too cavalier about this single most important contribution they make to their children at birth.

For the past several years, I have been studying the emotional and psychological impact of names, names of people, products and companies. This research has shown that names given things or people can have powerful effects on the preferences others show toward those things or persons.

The research, as applied here to thousands of names eliminates intuition and guesswork which can be misleading and sometimes dangerous in their consequences. Instead, it relies on straightforward logic and experimental data. The survey results represent the opinions of hundreds of people on what names mean to them.

Two Approaches for Using this Book

There are two different ways in which this book can help you make the decision of what to name your new child. The first approach is for you to start with a list of three to five names that you like. Because of tradition, or for other reasons, your child's name may have to begin with a certain letter. Even when your choices have been limited, you can use this book to help you pick the best choice.

The second approach is when you have no idea what name to select. This approach gives you more freedom, but the added freedom makes the ultimate decision more difficult.

In our studies, we have identified six major characteristic groups under which a name can be catagorized: successful, moral, healthy, warm, cheerful, masculine-feminine. Building upon this foundation, extensive surveys were conducted to rate a very large sample of names. The survey results provide specific numbers for each of the six major characteristics of a name.

To select a baby's name, parents must first decide what qualities or characteristics they value the most and would like to have their child project. Do they, for instance, wish to emphasize an image of success (which, in our ratings, also includes connotations of ambition, intelligence and creativity)? If so, they simply would review names in Chapters Five and Twelve that have the highest ratings on success. They would select a few of those names and try them out with friends or relatives to test reactions and to make a final selection.

Other Considerations

One other consideration in making a final choice might be the way in which the sounds of the first and last names harmonize. You should consider the initials of the child, and if the initials mean something, maybe those names should be eliminated. For example, if your surname is O'Reilly, if you name your son Bob, the initials B.O. will haunt him his entire life. Also many parents give their child a seamingly cute name which can cause their child unlimited teasing at school. For example two young girls were named Penelope "Penny" Stamp and Candice "Candy" Barr. Recently a young boy was named Zachary "Zach" Mann, leaving him vulnerable to the taunt "Zach PacMan," based on a video game with that name. Parents should consider the nicknames that their children will be given, and how that nickname will sound with their surname.

Recently, some acquaintances of mine were about to have a baby girl. They knew about my studies and wanted to know about the intended name for their baby. Since a grandmother on one side of the family and an aunt on the other side were both named Aida, that was the name they had picked.

I described my experimental findings and showed them how, according to objective survey data, the name Aida was not a good choice for their baby. Connotations for Aida (18, 45, 15, 38, 23, 40) given in Chapter Eleven show the reasons I tried to steer them away from that name. Aida connotes extremely low success, barely average morality, extremely low health, below average warmth, extremely low cheerfulness, and lack of femininity.

The example I cite is hardly unusual. Parents often name their babies in an accidental fashion, using names of favorite television personalities, movie stars, favorite friends and important figures from their past, or loved relatives. Worse yet, parents sometimes select outmoded and awkward names for their infants out of a sense of obligation to influential and older members of the family.

The personality and emotional makeup of the admired or loved person is associated with that person's name. So, a hidden and mistaken assumption is that the baby who is given the valued person's name will somehow inherit that person's admirable characteristics as well.

Let us say you love your grandfather Hank and decide to name your newborn son after him. True, the name Hank will probably elicit many warm and loving associations for you. But, will it have a similar effect on others? Will your son, as he [[es through life, get loving reactions from others simply because of his name? The safe answer is that this is very unlikely. Our personal associations with names of specific persons we know or admire are not likely to match associations of others to the same names.

These are some of the less serious problems which arise when parents use personal associations to name a child. More damaging consequences result when parents try to make an intellectual or artistic statement in naming an infant. Imagine the poor second-born named Beta because the parent is impressed with his own scholarship. Or, picture the numerous difficulties encountered by a person "artistically and spontaneously" named Wednesday for the day she was conceived.

A Boy Named Sue

[Johnny Cash recorded a song titled *A Boy Named Sue* back in the 1960s. The name got the boy into a lot of fist fights and made him tough. People are still giving their sons female, or other awkward, names. The following names were obtained from birth certificates of boys: Ann, Alice, Amber, Angela, Angel, Babe, Bunny, Bunny Ray, Cobra, Demon, Denim, Dutchboy, Fresno, Fern, Giant, Harmony, Her, Jane, Love, Lovie, Magnum, Male, Marguerite, Mom and Pitbull. Examples of inappropriate names given girls (obtained from the same source) were: Beauty, Brad, Bran, Brazil, Breezy, Bunny, Burgundy, Christmas, Cutie, Daiquiri, Dandy, Dave, Disney, Dug, Farm, Frank, Garbo, Italy and Joe.

Parents who select such outrageous names for their children, thinking that these are humorous, rebellious, artistic or intellectual, do a great disservice to their offspring. There is a considerable amount of research evidence pointing to an association between unusual and unpleasant characteristics of names and psychological problems. Thus, even though definite cause and effect relationships are not yet established, the evidence suggests strongly that those with more unusual names are more likely to have psychological problems.

The majority of parents, of course, do not go to the extremes noted above. However, most parents do in fact rely on intuition and guesswork. This book suggests that the haphazard method used to select names be replaced, or modified, by a more scientific approach.

Psychologically sophisticated readers probably have felt that intuitively selected children's names were unsatisfactory. But, until now, they had no systematic and objective data bank to use for selecting names. Those of you who already have felt this need will hopefully find the following pages refreshing, stimulating and helpful. In using our naming approach, you can proceed with confidence, knowing that the name you select for your child will impart certain clearly defined positive qualities.

Chapter Two

Changing Your Name

Darth Vader, Christie Brinkley, John Chancellor. These names instantly bring images into your mind. So does your name.

Sometimes, the characteristics implied by a name are consistent with the qualities we have, or those we wish to project. Unfortunately, and more commonly, our names give off impressions about ourselves that are inconsistent with our personalities or the characteristics we have worked hard to develop and seek to project.

A significant portion of the population is experiencing difficulties with given names. In a recent survey I conducted with a group of 255 male and female young adults, for instance, one out of six indicated they wished they had a different first name. An astounding 58 percent said they had considered various first name substitutes and produced one to three names which they preferred to their own.

I have received telephone calls and letters from many who reported they lived with awkward, difficult and embarrassing names well into adulthood, suffering humiliation, job bias and many daily discomforts because of those names. In some instances, clumsy or strange-sounding names led to open ridicule at work or while making presentations to various groups. Difficulties were encountered also in social situations or during initial encounters with members of the opposite sex. For example, imagine the numerous and lifelong problems encountered by men named Jack Daniels and Tom Collins. Or, think of the countless gibes targeted at a man named Nicolas

Vick, or Nick Vick.

Despite the ever-present and powerful impact of our names on our social lives and careers, and despite the high incidence of unsatisfactory names, most people fail to do anything about their unsuitable names. Major exceptions are those in the entertainment industry. People who make a living as singers, musicians, movie actors or artists are indeed more aware of the impression or aura created by a name and take on names more suited to the public image they wish to project.

For others, however, a name change appears to cause considerable difficulty. The randomness and guesswork in the search for alternative new names is disturbing and leads to hesitation and doubt. The typical book on names does not seem to be of much help, since for the most part, such books simply give the national origins of specific names, name meanings or guesses about qualities that might be associated with a name.

In addition, the actual mechanics of going through a legal name change are unknown to most. Because of apprehension about a name change, together with the anticipated effort in legalizing a new name, many people retain the bothersome and even handicapping names given them.

Survey Results

Even the daring who overcome hesitation and doubt and select a name they like better, often fail to realize their desired objectives. A friend who is a highly accomplished painter and is beginning to make a name for herself in the art world mentioned that she had settled on the new name Lola as a replacement of her given name, Jacqueline. Using the ratings for both names given in Chapter Eleven, I showed her that Jacqueline (103, 55, 91, 75, 70, 22), her original and given name, was far more appropriate than Lola (19, 20, 38, 45, 35, 36) if she wished to make a generally more positive impression as a professional.

Notice that the ratings for Jacqueline and Lola show Jacqueline connotes greater success, morality, health, warmth and cheerfulness than Lola. In addition, Jacqueline is judged as more feminine than Lola. Thus, my friend was mistaken in her intuitive choice of Lola as a better name to create an intelligent, creative, and generally artistic image.

The Solution May Be Your Middle Name

Our approach to the selection of a new name is illustrated best by considering two of the easier ways in which this can be accomplished. The first of these involves using your middle name instead of your given name. Since most people have both a first and a middle name, it is a relatively easy matter to look up both in our tables and decide which one of the two is more suited to the image you want to project.

Let's say your name is Clarence Eric Jones and you consider a healthy image (which within our ratings includes being physically healthy, popular, athletic, good-looking, confident and assertive) the single most desirable quality you would like to project. You will find the following two sets of ratings in Chapter Four for your first and middle names. Numerical scores in each row represent successful, moral, healthy, warm, cheerful and masculine qualities, listed left to right.

Clarence (first name): 59 61 30 36 (23) 63

Eric (middle name): 68 (20) [89] 61 [95] (84)♂

Circled numbers indicate a very low score. I have circled every number under 30. The box around the high numbers indicates an extremely high score. Scores over 70 are boxed. Scores of 50 are average and scores typically range from zero to 100, with values approaching 100 representing extremely high scores on any characteristic and those approaching zero representing extremely low scores. The male symbol ♂ indicates a very masculine name. A ♀ (female symbol) is used to note very feminine names.

Comparison of the two rows shows that Eric has stronger success, health, warmth, cheerfulness and masculinity connotations than Clarence. Eric, though, is weaker than Clarence in its connotation of morality. Remembering that your most important concern is to project health, you will find Eric to be far more suitable–with a rating of 89 on healthy which is far greater than the corresponding rating of 30 for Clarence. As a bonus, a choice of Eric will also give you a more successful, warm, cheerful and masculine image, resulting overall in a considerably more favorable image than Clarence.

Knowing all this, you may decide to go ahead and use the following version of your name: C. Eric Jones. You would simply have to request and insist that your friends, relatives, and co-workers call you by your middle name. Those who you meet for the first time would get to know you as Eric and you would write your name as C. Eric Jones in correspondence to insure that you are known as Eric.

Nicknames

A second relatively simple way to accomplish a name change is to become aware of the connotations of your given name and nickname(s). I recently met an accountant whose first name was Andrew. When I called his office, I was surprised to discover the receptionist refer to him as Andy. This meant that he used his nickname, Andy, at work and in his professional relationships with clients. I was surprised because I knew the name Andy was a weaker name than Andrew, especially when used in professional situations. Compare the following two sets of ratings which also have been taken from Chapter Four:

Andrew (given name):	[89]	[71]	70	55	38	[74]
Andy (nickname):	45	44	64	59	66	70

Andrew is much stronger than Andy in connoting success and morality. It is roughly comparable to Andy with respect to health, warmth, and masculinity, but is weaker than Andy in cheerfulness. So, if my acquaintance, the accountant, were to decide to use his given name Andrew, he would have a significant image gain at the cost of a less cheerful-sounding name. Cheerfulness, however, would seem to be only marginally important in the professional world of accounting and the image gain would thus outstrip the image-associated loss in cheerfulness.

Many of us are called by our nicknames. Strangers sometimes call me Al (which I've always disliked) and friends and relatives call me Albert. When our study was completed, I noted the following two sets of ratings and understood my intuitive aversion to Al.

Albert (given name):	54	61	45	66	50	64
Al (nickname):	28	23	60	49	65	76♂

Since these ratings represent successful, moral, healthy, warm, cheerful and masculine, left to right, Albert is stronger than Al in connoting success, morality and warmth. Al is stronger concerning health, cheerfulness and masculinity. But success, morality and warmth are more important to me than the others, which explains my preference for Albert.

Let's take one more example. Consider the name Elizabeth and compare it with the nickname Liz. Ratings for these, taken from Chapter Eleven, are as follows:

Elizabeth (given name):	76	86	64	73	57	22♀
Liz (nickname):	56	47	49	41	67	35

Remembering that these ratings represent successful, moral, healthy, warm, cheerful and masculine-feminine from left to right, the comparison clearly favors Elizabeth. The nickname connotes less success, morality, health, warmth, and femininity (since low scores in the last column represent femininity, which is the opposite of masculinity). Liz only excels in connoting greater cheerfulness.

Someone who goes by the nickname Liz would thus have to decide what is important to her– to appear cheerful or to appear successful, moral, healthy, warm, and feminine. I would think that most women would prefer Elizabeth to Liz once they knew the differences in connotations between the two.

In my approach to name choices a possible change of name would begin with greater name awareness.

Start by examining your given first and middle names and compare connotations these have with those of various nicknames (or even alternative name spellings). In a significant amount of cases, a comparison would produce a more suitable name selection from among various given names.

If, however, none of the given names or their variations is satisfactory, then, one might consider a name change involving completely new first, middle and/or last names. In doing so, you would first need to decide on the most desired name connotation, followed perhaps by the second and third most important connotations.

If you want a name that will be an asset in professional life and desire to emphasize success, followed by health and cheerfulness, you would proceed to Chapter Five which provides a list of the most successful-sounding names for men and Chapter Twelve for a similar list of the most successful names for women. Among these top-rated names on success, you would find many which also have high ratings on health and cheerfulness.

Narrow your choices down to a short list of five or six and then try these out with friends and relatives. Let them know you are considering a name change and see how they react to you with the new names.

The key to a successful name change, then, is to have a rational and logical basis for selecting a new name. Given the extensive data in our various chapters, your initial efforts are bound to be rewarded, since the names you select will have connotations that you desire. Favorable feedback from others should give you enough confidence and motivate you to overcome the hurdles in going through a legal name change.

Chapter Three

How to Use the Tables

In the rest of this book, most tables have the same format: Rows in the tables represent names and columns represent characteristics. Chapter Four contains survey results for all the male names and Chapter Eleven provides the results for female names. Remaining chapters contain various lists of the findings given in Chapters Four and Eleven.

Let us say, however, that for your starting point you simply wish to know the connotations of a given name such as Hannah. You would use Chapter Eleven where female names are arranged alphabetically and find the name Hannah together with the following row of numbers:

Hannah 67 [96] 51 [86] 55 30

All six numbers are based on scales which have average values of 50. As a score increases from 50, it shows a higher level of the characteristic. Scores approaching 100 (or, for only a small fraction of the names, those exceeding 100) show an extremely significant and high level of the characteristic. For most practical purposes, scores as high as 70 imply a significantly high level of a particular characteristic and those exceeding 70 imply even greater levels of that characteristic. Scores over 70 on the charts are noted with a box ☐.

In a similar way, as a score decreases below 50, it shows a lower level of the characteristic. Scores approaching zero (or, for only a small fraction of the names, those below zero) show an extremely significant and low level of the characteristic. Once again, for most practical purposes, scores as low as 30 indicate a significantly low level of a particular characteristic and those less than 30 imply even lower levels of the characteristic. Scores below 30 are marked with a circle ◯.

Take another look at the six numbers we have for Hannah. Remember that in all tables, the number in the first column represents the degree of **Success** implied by a name, the number in the second column represents implied **Morality**, that in the third column represents **Health**, the fourth column represents **Warmth**, the fifth column indicates **Cheerfulness**, and finally the sixth column signifies **Masculinity-Femininity**, with high scores (above 50) for masculinity and low scores (below 50) for femininity.

The row of six numbers given above for Hannah thus shows that this name connotes a reasonably high degree of success, an extremely high degree of morality, an average degree of health, a very high degree of warmth, an average degree of cheerfulness, and a reasonably high degree of femininity.

Essentially, then, Chapters Four and Eleven provide dictionaries of connotations of male and female names, respectively. Names are listed in alphabetical order and you should be able to find the list of six connotations for most names of interest.

To quickly discover the list of names which have the highest connotations of **Success**, turn to Chapter Five for male names. You would find the names James, Madison, Charles, Alexander, Kenneth or Thomas at the top of the list with extremely high ratings on success. In comparison, the names Jethro, Jock, Jose, Elmo, Angel, Rufus, Bud and Butch have extremely low success ratings.

Alternatively, supposing you wish to identify female names with very high connotations of morality. In that case you would use the table in Chapter Thirteen which contains female names with very high ratings on morality. That list begins with the names Prudence, Hope, Esther, Agnes, Abigail, Emma and Cornelia which connote extremely high levels of morality. In comparison, the names Goldie, Daphne, Tiffany, Brandy, Mandy, Farrah, Roxanne and Trixie connote extremely low levels of morality.

The remaining chapters are similarly organized. Chapters Seven and Fourteen contain names with high connotations of health; Chapters Eight and Fifteen contains names with connotations of warmth; Chapters Nine and Sixteen provide names with extreme ratings on cheerfulness and Chapters Ten and Seventeen list names with strong ratings of masculinity and femininity.

Let us say, for instance, you want a name for a baby boy to connote very high masculinity. In that case, you would turn to the Chapter Ten and find that the names Conan, Buck, Duke, Rex, Chad, or Robert have very high masculinity ratings. Chapter Seventeen identifies female names with extremely low masculinity (that is, extremely high femininity) ratings such as Bunny, Zsa Zsa, Barbie, Fifi and so forth.

Keep in mind that a name, through its connotations, says something about the child or adult. Let us say a child, because of an unfortunate name choice, gives off the impression of being cheerless and unhappy.

Then, quite possibly, the name can lead friends and teachers, or even strangers, to view and treat him in ways which will have an undesirable effect on the direction of his personality development.

Just as a parent would not have her child dressed or groomed so as to make the wrong kind of impression, by the same token, I doubt that a parent would deliberately wish her child to have a name which projects the wrong kind of image. So, to be safe, a parent can select a name which does not have undesirable connotations. Better yet, the parent can select a name so as to highlight a desired set of positive connotations. The following tables should help parents make such systematic searches of names.

In a similar way, someone desiring a name change can first decide which positive characteristics he wishes to highlight in his new name. He then can search through our tables to identify several names with the desired positive connotations.

The simplest cases are choices of nicknames versus given names. Take a look, for instance, at the ratings for Donald and Donny in Chapter Four. The ratings show that Donald is far superior to Donny in several aspects. So, someone who is named Donald but has been called Donny by family and friends can insist that business associates call him Donald. With some effort, he could even get most of his relatives and friends to call him Donald. With this simple shift to Donald, the image portrayed by his name could improve substantially and connote greater degrees of success, morality and cheerfulness.

A final guide to the use of the tables rests on the recognition that our key words for each of the six basic characteristics serve only as summary terms. For example, say you wish to have a name that connotes intelligence and creativity. Superficially, our six characteristics do not seem to contain those qualities. However, if you look at the list of characteristics subsumed under **Success**, you will find it to include "ambitious," "intelligent" and "creative." So, it is important to always keep in mind the group of characteristics representing each column of scores in our tables. For your convenience, these groups are reproduced below.

Successful: successful, ambitious, intelligent, creative

Moral: moral, obedient, respectful, religious, loyal, trustworthy

Healthy: healthy, popular, athletic, good-looking, confident, assertive

Warm: warm, loving, caring, kind, generous

Cheerful: cheerful, playful, curious, friendly, humorous

Masculine-feminine: You know them when you see them.

BOYS
NAMES

The Name Game

	Success	Morality	Health	Warmth	Cheerful	Male - Female
AARON	62	52	68	61	49	70
ABBOT	(20)	36	36	(16)	43	58
ABDUL	51	44	44	32	36	(82)♂
ABE	39	58	39	58	48	(77)♂
ABEL	52	[99]	37	59	(20)	66
ABNER	(18)	46	35	35	42	59
ABRAHAM	[85]	[106]	38	63	(23)	70
ABRAM	49	61	40	57	41	68
ACE	36	(14)	62	35	53	(73)♂
ADAM	[93]	55	70	55	55	(76)♂
ADDISON	[76]	60	57	44	58	(71)♂
ADLAI	50	51	39	43	45	50
ADOLPH	[84]	(22)	42	(1)	(-6)	(76)♂
ADONIS	31	31	35	(18)	(22)	59
ADRIAN	56	43	58	54	56	55
AL	(28)	(23)	60	49	65	(76)♂
ALAN	[84]	58	54	[72]	45	69
ALASTAIR	65	58	40	46	39	53
ALBERT	54	61	45	66	50	64

KEY: Least - ○ Most - □ Masculine - ♂

The Name Game

	Success	Morality	Health	Warmth	Cheerful	Male - Female
ALDEN	[79]	64	40	46	44	59
ALDO	(17)	(24)	(29)	(13)	(21)	63
ALDRIDGE	31	(29)	35	(23)	(21)	62
ALEC	67	44	65	50	65	(72)♂
ALEX	62	44	62	49	56	65
ALEXANDER	[102]	65	60	52	(28)	(71)♂
ALEXIS	55	55	59	40	46	49
ALFONSO	48	43	44	44	52	70
ALFRED	63	[93]	(26)	56	(23)	57
ALGER	47	45	30	32	(29)	53
ALGERNON	35	31	(27)	(20)	(17)	60
ALI	47	43	42	46	55	63
ALLARD	40	40	39	34	36	57
ALONZO	(17)	(27)	42	(28)	37	68
ALPHONSE	50	51	56	48	54	64
ALTON	56	52	38	45	43	70
ALVIN	35	46	34	47	47	57
AMBROSE	35	(25)	35	(21)	(22)	56
AMORY	63	[81]	34	[73]	49	62

KEY: Least - ◯ Most - □ Masculine - ♂

The Name Game

	Success	Morality	Health	Warmth	Cheerful	Male - Female
AMOS	31	[73]	30	61	62	63
ANDRE	63	(15)	[74]	41	44	(75) ♂
ANDREW	[89]	[71]	70	55	38	(74) ♂
ANDY	45	44	64	59	66	70
ANGEL	(2)	31	30	(29)	30	48
ANGELO	38	56	58	63	62	(76) ♂
ANGUS	58	47	34	34	34	(71) ♂
ANSEL	64	66	37	51	41	57
ANSON	62	63	55	[79]	57	65
ANTHONY	68	66	67	61	58	(77) ♂
ANTOINE	55	44	44	48	47	56
ANTONIO	47	56	66	62	57	(75) ♂
ARCHIBALD	59	[86]	(8)	(29)	(19)	58
ARCHIE	31	40	36	42	63	68
ARDEN	50	48	49	47	48	57
ARIEL	49	56	43	44	43	47
ARMAND	70	60	49	52	51	(71) ♂
ARMIN	(29)	34	(26)	(22)	(13)	62
ARMONDO	38	40	39	(10)	(27)	70

KEY: Least - ○ Most - □ Masculine - ♂

The Name Game

	Success	Morality	Health	Warmth	Cheerful	Male - Female
ARNIE	37	44	43	44	55	59
ARNOLD	(16)	54	(12)	48	(20)	56
ART	48	41	41	37	49	65
ARTHUR	[75]	58	48	50	30	65
ARTIE	45	50	42	56	[71]	63
ARVIN	35	36	(23)	(25)	(23)	60
ASHBY	68	65	59	61	53	65
ASHER	51	43	50	45	43	60
ASHFORD	[73]	54	58	44	48	70
ASHLEY	55	52	61	63	54	47
AUBREY	35	44	37	(26)	30	50
AUGIE	(21)	(28)	31	(27)	36	53
AUGUST	49	57	56	36	37	55
AUGUSTINE	44	44	42	40	36	55
AUSTIN	67	36	[72]	42	44	70
AVERIL	31	37	(25)	(17)	(26)	54
AVERILL	41	49	(27)	40	33	52
AVERY	47	43	36	30	40	54
AVRAM	42	48	41	40	43	68

KEY: Least - ○ Most - □ Masculine - ♂

	Success	Morality	Health	Warmth	Cheerful	Male - Female
AXEL	57	43	57	43	51	59
BAIRD	59	46	51	51	45	63
BALDWIN	56	51	49	45	51	61
BALFOUR	38	44	31	30	34	51
BANCROFT	60	45	40	44	47	64
BARCLAY	68	58	63	45	44	66
BARNABY	51	53	33	42	42	66
BARNETT	50	42	56	59	48	73 ♂
BARNEY	(24) ○	(26) ○	30	31	33	72 ♂
BARON	67	52	64	42	33	73 ♂
BARRETT	63	58	67	56	52	68
BARRY	[72] □	47	64	65	70	68
BART	35	47	53	36	42	78 ♂
BARTHOLEMEW	[88] □	[93] □	(29) ○	49	(12) ○	58
BARTON	57	50	54	49	41	72 ♂
BASIL	[79] □	[72] □	34	48	37	56
BAXTER	69	49	67	56	55	78 ♂
BAYARD	41	46	36	52	39	58
BEAU	59	52	[72] □	54	57	73 ♂

KEY: Least - ○ Most - □ Masculine - ♂

The Name Game

	Success	Morality	Health	Warmth	Cheerful	Male - Female
BELLAMY	53	46	34	38	41	59
BEN	[74]	[79]	55	[71]	67	(76)♂
BENEDICT	54	64	42	40	40	66
BENJAMIN	[89]	[74]	44	55	40	(75)♂
BENNY	35	42	34	32	54	62
BENSON	68	60	47	51	51	(76)♂
BENTLEY	68	56	42	42	42	59
BENTON	60	53	65	56	50	(72)♂
BERN	39	45	40	40	40	60
BERNARD	40	[73]	30	41	(21)	68
BERT	42	44	39	36	44	67
BERTRAM	47	43	(21)	49	37	59
BEVAN	40	36	42	40	34	56
BILL	67	45	[80]	54	65	(86)♂
BILLY	(28)	40	56	47	[74]	(74)♂
BING	40	37	48	39	50	54
BIRCH	39	42	47	39	44	60
BIRNEY	37	39	40	36	46	63
BJORN	54	43	[73]	44	43	(72)♂

KEY: Least - ○ Most - □ Masculine - ♂

	Success	Morality	Health	Warmth	Cheerful	Male - Female
BLADE	42	45	62	38	45	♂○76
BLAINE	59	38	57	37	44	65
BLAIR	65	39	67	46	50	54
BLAKE	□82	○23	□86	34	48	♂○79
BO	○22	40	59	38	57	♂○72
BOB	□76	61	□76	□73	63	♂○81
BOGART	52	46	36	36	44	♂○71
BOND	□73	43	66	38	40	♂○73
BOONE	35	39	47	47	52	♂○71
BORG	41	44	58	38	33	♂○82
BORIS	○16	48	○21	○21	○21	♂○75
BOYD	44	46	47	39	41	70
BRAD	□90	45	□91	49	65	♂○79
BRADEN	□79	58	65	51	57	♂○72
BRADFORD	□77	66	67	48	53	♂○78
BRADLEY	□71	58	70	61	65	♂○73
BRADSHAW	□72	58	60	47	57	♂○79
BRADY	□72	49	70	49	60	70
BRANDON	□78	43	□77	64	63	♂○73

KEY: Least - ○ Most - □ Masculine - ♂

The Name Game

	Success	Morality	Health	Warmth	Cheerful	Male - Female
BRENDAN	[73]	41	66	52	46	68
BRENT	67	46	[73]	56	58	(71)♂
BRENTON	[75]	58	61	53	51	(73)♂
BRETT	57	42	58	45	60	(76)♂
BREWSTER	49	42	49	36	48	66
BRIAN	[71]	56	[85]	69	[80]	(79)♂
BRICE	63	53	[72]	60	58	70
BRIGHAM	65	[71]	53	59	53	65
BROCK	40	42	50	40	37	70
BRODERICK	66	65	63	59	51	(72)♂
BRODIE	49	44	49	42	56	(73)♂
BRONSON	58	40	67	37	42	(80)♂
BRUCE	57	(23)	[79]	44	59	(82)♂
BRUNO	(11)	(10)	45	(4)	(14)	(82)♂
BRYANT	64	58	66	57	52	(71)♂
BUCK	(28)	(10)	[95]	(8)	59	(91)♂
BUD	(1)	(23)	46	30	49	(79)♂
BURGESS	58	58	41	59	48	64
BURKE	63	62	50	50	49	(78)♂

KEY: Least - ○ Most - □ Masculine - ♂

The Name Game

	Success	Morality	Health	Warmth	Cheerful	Male - Female
BURL	38	41	43	41	52	75 ♂
BURT	42	39	54	52	50	76 ♂
BURTON	70	58	59	50	60	73 ♂
BUTCH	○ -8	○ 13	39	○ 4	○ 17	84 ♂
BYRON	□ 72	55	59	49	44	68
CAESAR	52	46	42	33	42	72 ♂
CAL	45	48	56	48	56	66
CALDWELL	68	39	57	41	36	67
CALHOUN	46	45	31	40	45	64
CALVERT	58	53	36	46	42	66
CALVIN	□ 76	55	□ 71	58	65	75 ♂
CAMDEN	□ 71	54	65	49	51	66
CAMERON	66	54	55	41	57	68
CARL	66	33	68	53	62	69
CARLETON	70	48	60	50	29	68
CARLIN	47	49	44	50	52	67
CARLISLE	□ 73	55	57	54	49	59
CARLOS	○ 23	36	37	40	41	77 ♂
CARNEY	45	33	39	50	55	64

KEY: Least - ○ Most - □ Masculine - ♂

The Name Game

	Success	Morality	Health	Warmth	Cheerful	Male - Female
CARR	62	45	55	43	40	60
CARROLL	47	53	42	60	49	46
CARSON	56	45	59	50	59	69
CARTER	81 □	73 □	56	55	53	72 ♂
CARVER	57	51	53	49	43	68
CARY	58	52	74 □	65	66	63
CASEY	63	38	69	59	80 □	66
CASPER	46	43	45	34	38	50
CASSIDY	64	39	64	54	57	68
CASSIUS	55	56	51	40	37	68
CEASAR	49	44	43	14 ○	7 ○	71 ♂
CECIL	39	60	26 ○	52	48	51
CEDRIC	42	45	47	29 ○	45	65
CHAD	81 □	52	98 □	56	79 □	86 ♂
CHADWICK	65	57	55	41	40	71 ♂
CHALMERS	55	43	34	36	30	55
CHANDLER	76 □	60	73 □	50	56	75 ♂
CHANEY	65	44	55	54	45	63
CHANNING	62	49	63	52	49	58

KEY: Least - ○ Most - □ Masculine - ♂

The Name Game

	Success	Morality	Health	Warmth	Cheerful	Male - Female
CHAPMAN	55	43	51	50	42	66
CHARLES	□105	□79	68	69	55	♂78
CHARLIE	42	30	56	51	□91	69
CHARLTON	66	52	66	48	50	70
CHASE	□71	51	63	46	50	♂75
CHAUNCEY	49	50	43	45	52	57
CHESTER	64	□73	○28	51	32	61
CHET	○29	○14	52	○28	52	70
CHIC	○19	○14	○23	○28	42	50
CHICO	○15	○21	○26	○29	45	69
CHILTON	46	49	35	33	34	62
CHIP	32	31	57	41	69	69
CHRIS	51	44	64	52	63	65
CHRISTIAN	55	□74	61	□72	53	59
CHRISTOPHER	□88	63	□80	59	59	♂75
CHUCK	57	38	□86	47	□75	♂83
CID	37	○28	34	38	45	63
CLARENCE	59	61	30	36	○23	63
CLARK	□81	□82	56	61	38	♂76

KEY: Least - ○ Most - □ Masculine - ♂

The Name Game

	Success	Morality	Health	Warmth	Cheerful	Male - Female
CLAUDE	50	42	31	51	42	66
CLAUS	33	(28)	41	(20)	(20)	64
CLAY	63	49	[80]	48	58	(76)♂
CLAYBORNE	57	53	47	49	39	67
CLAYTON	56	30	53	33	38	70
CLEVELAND	46	60	44	49	50	63
CLIFF	53	48	67	44	51	(77)♂
CLIFFORD	53	52	60	48	42	(74)♂
CLIFTON	54	52	49	56	50	68
CLINT	56	46	[71]	45	42	(80)♂
CLINTON	[71]	50	63	36	42	(74)♂
CLIVE	43	43	32	41	44	57
CLYDE	(27)	37	32	(29)	36	67
CODY	53	50	66	56	66	(76)♂
COLBERT	55	43	54	33	34	59
COLBY	[93]	41	[84]	41	50	(80)♂
COLE	51	58	49	48	53	69
COLEMAN	55	47	53	51	54	65
COLLIER	61	54	57	51	41	56

KEY: Least - ( ) Most - [ ] Masculine - ♂

The Name Game

	Success	Morality	Health	Warmth	Cheerful	Male - Female
COLLIN	89 (Most)	47	85 (Most)	44	63	78 (Masculine)
COLTON	67	57	73 (Most)	45	42	77 (Masculine)
CONAN	28 (Least)	46	60	23 (Least)	24 (Least)	94 (Masculine)
CONNOR	68	55	62	49	52	72 (Masculine)
CONRAD	89 (Most)	59	67	52	52	74 (Masculine)
CONROY	58	58	56	51	42	68
CONSTANTINE	56	56	35	47	31	60
COOPER	55	50	52	47	56	69
CORBETT	64	52	60	46	51	72 (Masculine)
COREY	56	50	60	51	52	68
CORNELIUS	51	72 (Most)	9 (Least)	25 (Least)	12 (Least)	59
CORNELL	65	60	50	56	51	63
CORY	49	46	59	56	69	63
COURTNEY	49	59	51	54	65	55
COWAN	57	48	47	39	40	66
CRAIG	76 (Most)	35	94 (Most)	48	65	81 (Masculine)
CRANDALL	60	53	37	44	38	61
CRAWFORD	61	50	55	54	39	72 (Masculine)
CREIGHTON	44	41	41	25 (Least)	26 (Least)	67

KEY: Least - ○ Most - □ Masculine - ♂

	Success	Morality	Health	Warmth	Cheerful	Male - Female
CROMWELL	59	58	50	43	47	66
CROSBY	62	58	53	58	58	69
CULLEN	57	58	54	42	45	64
CULVER	47	52	41	36	40	65
CURT	55	53	67	51	59	(72) ♂
CURTIS	68	(21)	[82]	39	61	(72) ♂
CYRIL	56	63	32	52	(27)	55
CYRUS	52	67	43	43	37	59
DAG	(27)	(26)	42	32	40	(73) ♂
DALE	44	56	48	44	46	66
DALLAS	51	38	62	(27)	42	(78) ♂
DALTON	[73]	50	54	50	42	(73) ♂
DAMIAN	67	51	69	51	52	(71) ♂
DAMON	57	(12)	[85]	(19)	35	(82) ♂
DAN	69	48	[76]	44	62	(76) ♂
DANA	49	45	63	64	69	48
DANIEL	[74]	66	[73]	[73]	[83]	70
DANTE	45	36	39	30	38	66
DARBY	46	50	53	62	66	59

KEY: Least - ○ Most - □ Masculine - ♂

The Name Game

	Success	Morality	Health	Warmth	Cheerful	Male - Female
DARCY	68	48	47	59	45	46
DARIUS	57	50	47	42	40	65
DARNELL	34	27 ○	48	31	48	67
DARREL	67	28 ○	71 □	48	70	78 ♂
DARREN	67	31	77 □	49	65	77 ♂
DARWIN	56	61	29 ○	50	39	61
DAVE	64	38	68	50	68	76 ♂
DAVID	92 □	54	85 □	72 □	73 □	81 ♂
DAVIS	70	60	65	44	51	70
DAVY	34	44	43	54	71 □	65
DEAN	67	49	80 □	51	46	80 ♂
DEDRICK	45	48	48	42	44	69
DELANEY	58	56	55	63	55	64
DELBERT	40	45	18 ○	43	32	57
DELMORE	45	46	34	36	35	61
DEMETRIUS	49	38	41	25 ○	30	62
DENNIS	71 □	58	65	65	80 □	72 ♂
DENNISON	60	61	58	49	43	70
DENNY	39	52	54	56	72 □	66

KEY: Least - ○ Most - □ Masculine - ♂

The Name Game

	Success	Morality	Health	Warmth	Cheerful	Male - Female
DENTON	50	50	45	43	46	66
DEREK	57	30	[85]	44	66	(81)♂
DERRICK	67	50	[74]	55	[72]	(78)♂
DESMOND	50	49	50	49	48	66
DEVIN	58	32	55	(20)	53	68
DEVLIN	41	40	44	41	41	67
DEXTER	45	46	43	37	54	(72)♂
DICK	[72]	49	56	44	59	(75)♂
DIETRICH	58	57	50	32	41	67
DILLON	66	50	69	42	56	(79)♂
DIRK	40	42	51	37	38	(72)♂
DMITRI	48	44	58	53	45	67
DOMINIC	51	37	47	46	50	68
DON	70	51	64	58	66	(72)♂
DONAHUE	64	58	64	46	45	68
DONALD	[81]	66	42	55	[71]	70
DONNELLY	69	57	64	54	59	63
DONNY	33	46	43	49	59	63
DONOVAN	70	63	55	58	69	69

KEY: Least - ○ Most - □ Masculine - ♂

	Success	Morality	Health	Warmth	Cheerful	Male - Female
DORIAN	63	48	34	41	31	52
DOUG	43	37	63	43	56	(75)♂
DOUGLAS	[84]	61	64	63	53	(76)♂
DRAKE	[77]	47	[85]	(22)	(26)	(81)♂
DREW	[92]	66	[89]	68	[73]	(75)♂
DRYDEN	48	52	45	43	35	65
DUANE	39	36	43	30	42	69
DUDLEY	31	44	37	36	49	57
DUKE	49	31	[85]	(22)	41	(89)♂
DUNCAN	54	59	47	68	70	68
DUSTIN	[77]	38	58	45	49	(71)♂
DWAYNE	51	45	45	47	55	66
DWIGHT	44	45	53	(28)	33	70
DYLAN	55	45	61	51	48	(75)♂
EARL	45	59	40	38	(20)	64
ED	38	43	40	31	32	(71)♂
EDDIE	37	31	65	63	[90]	69
EDGAR	44	37	(12)	(27)	(20)	64
EDISON	57	51	37	44	37	60

KEY: Least - ( ) Most - [ ] Masculine - ♂

The Name Game

	Success	Morality	Health	Warmth	Cheerful	Male - Female
EDMUND	[79]	[75]	41	48	44	65
EDSEL	(26)	48	(20)	40	(19)	55
EDWARD	[92]	[82]	66	63	40	(74)♂
EDWIN	62	[78]	(22)	49	(21)	56
EFRAM	34	(25)	32	(11)	(17)	59
EGAN	43	48	37	44	40	58
EGBERT	38	49	(13)	36	(27)	53
ELDRIDGE	54	61	51	46	47	60
ELI	32	(28)	(19)	(29)	(24)	59
ELIAS	35	53	32	50	44	66
ELLIOT	[86]	[86]	(26)	55	54	58
ELLIS	64	57	61	59	62	69
ELLISON	54	54	52	57	54	68
ELLSWORTH	68	58	51	51	54	65
ELMER	(24)	[90]	(8)	65	40	57
ELMO	(8)	52	(19)	35	38	58
ELTON	41	44	36	37	54	65
ELVIS	43	39	46	37	55	62
ELWOOD	(20)	(29)	31	31	32	60

KEY: Least - ○ Most - □ Masculine - ♂

	Success	Morality	Health	Warmth	Cheerful	Male - Female
EMERY	59	54	48	44	46	63
EMIL	49	51	35	47	43	55
EMILIO	44	34	48	39	41	70
EMMANUEL	26 ○	46	33	38	51	61
EMMET	22 ○	35	27 ○	36	46	62
ENGELBERT	28 ○	50	16 ○	45	37	59
ENRICO	34	38	45	34	52	73 ○♂
ERHARD	49	45	35	30	23 ○	58
ERIC	68	20 ○	89 □	61	95 □	84 ○♂
ERIN	62	60	63	56	62	50
ERNEST	67	93 □	28 ○	52	17 ○	51
ERNIE	20 ○	46	28 ○	49	36	59
ERROL	63	50	55	46	48	68
ERWIN	30	45	35	42	47	59
ETHAN	54	61	43	49	35	60
ETIENNE	45	46	34	54	46	53
EUGENE	70	75 □	10 ○	42	42	47
EVAN	54	54	55	53	51	62
EVERETT	72 □	47	60	34	32	65

KEY: Least - 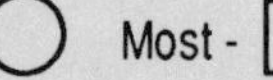 Most - □ Masculine - 

The Name Game

	Success	Morality	Health	Warmth	Cheerful	Male - Female
EZRA	33	70	(24)	49	34	56
FABIAN	61	35	[71]	42	42	63
FARLEY	44	60	37	49	58	58
FARRELL	54	57	58	61	55	60
FELIX	32	44	(27)	(26)	48	58
FERGUS	59	62	31	(28)	(29)	56
FERNANDO	(19)	37	35	(28)	42	♂72
FERRIS	56	34	50	35	54	66
FIELDING	66	58	55	41	48	64
FILBERT	43	[82]	(-1)	51	(10)	44
FILMORE	46	52	37	40	45	59
FITZGERALD	69	66	52	47	56	♂75
FITZPATRICK	[71]	67	63	54	54	♂75
FLEMING	55	48	42	48	44	57
FLETCHER	56	44	44	45	50	68
FLINT	47	45	65	37	53	♂81
FLOYD	70	[72]	(28)	51	32	58
FLYNN	54	49	53	53	59	66
FORBES	70	56	46	42	39	♂75

KEY: Least - ○ Most - □ Masculine - ♂

The Name Game

	Success	Morality	Health	Warmth	Cheerful	Male - Female
FORD	51	42	43	(22)	32	70
FORREST	68	50	54	39	48	64
FOSTER	44	39	42	(29)	(24)	68
FOWLER	51	42	32	32	35	66
FRANCIS	51	[78]	50	[81]	55	55
FRANCISCO	45	46	38	(27)	46	(71)♂
FRANK	[74]	37	[72]	38	54	(78)♂
FRANKLIN	[79]	[84]	(18)	52	(22)	59
FRAZER	49	31	43	(17)	(25)	66
FRED	47	55	(23)	61	33	70
FREDDY	(26)	41	45	35	54	69
FREDERICK	61	56	51	51	55	(72)♂
FRITZ	48	37	44	40	64	70
FULLER	63	56	49	46	38	61
GABRIEL	[71]	[79]	57	[76]	53	55
GALLAGHER	51	42	42	49	63	64
GALVIN	55	58	50	53	52	65
GARETH	58	56	61	61	51	(76)♂
GARFIELD	57	57	35	46	46	68

KEY: Least - ( ) Most - [ ] Masculine - ♂

The Name Game

	Success	Morality	Health	Warmth	Cheerful	Male - Female
GARLAND	43	62	37	45	40	51
GARNER	63	56	55	42	49	66
GARRETT	60	48	64	50	60	66
GARRICK	□ 72	54	67	51	57	♂ 79
GARSON	56	37	41	○ 28	35	69
GARTH	43	55	47	○ 26	36	70
GARVEY	54	45	55	41	48	♂ 74
GARVIN	35	36	○ 28	31	34	59
GARY	□ 72	38	□ 83	61	□ 93	♂ 79
GASTON	42	44	59	34	42	♂ 73
GAVIN	□ 72	69	54	39	44	♂ 73
GAYLORD	54	58	41	40	45	66
GENE	63	37	40	55	57	60
GEOFFREY	□ 83	□ 71	63	66	65	68
GEORGE	59	56	36	58	55	61
GEORGIO	51	○ 25	43	30	55	64
GERALD	46	58	44	30	53	♂ 72
GERARD	64	41	39	○ 25	○ 29	♂ 72
GERMAIN	45	40	47	45	46	66

KEY: Least - ○ Most - □ Masculine - ♂

The Name Game

	Success	Morality	Health	Warmth	Cheerful	Male - Female
GIFFORD	44	40	40	(26)	30	66
GILBERT	35	65	(18)	35	37	64
GILES	39	36	45	(29)	38	59
GILMORE	35	44	36	30	30	65
GILROY	33	42	(26)	43	41	58
GINO	(22)	(26)	65	41	57	(77) ♂
GIO	32	(24)	32	(18)	34	57
GIOVANNI	57	60	65	61	57	(73) ♂
GIUSEPPE	37	51	50	63	66	68
GLEN	[71]	61	[76]	69	67	(77) ♂
GLENDON	55	47	50	43	46	65
GODDARD	46	45	35	30	(26)	63
GODFREY	42	42	32	(25)	(15)	60
GORDON	61	58	48	55	41	64
GRADY	35	40	38	(27)	36	66
GRAHAM	[77]	[79]	56	66	52	68
GRANGER	55	57	49	56	46	(75) ♂
GRANT	[78]	49	[78]	48	58	(80) ♂
GRAYSON	63	66	67	59	60	(76) ♂

KEY: Least - ○ Most - □ Masculine - ♂

The Name Game

	Success	Morality	Health	Warmth	Cheerful	Male - Female
GREG	66	65	67	54	[74]	(78)♂
GREGOR	58	58	47	49	46	(74)♂
GREGORY	[85]	[71]	[89]	52	[74]	(84)♂
GRIFFIN	[71]	56	55	52	52	64
GRIFFITH	62	52	50	52	50	68
GRISWOLD	30	40	(26)	(23)	31	62
GROVER	(18)	(29)	(17)	(24)	40	54
GUIDO	30	32	(27)	34	38	69
GUILLERMO	36	40	41	42	42	(72)♂
GUNTHER	33	41	46	34	42	(74)♂
GUS	35	35	51	42	[73]	(71)♂
GUSTAVE	46	56	40	45	52	64
GUTHRIE	(28)	33	35	(26)	(25)	63
GUY	52	49	[76]	50	62	(72)♂
HADLEY	49	53	47	37	46	58
HAL	61	48	44	52	62	69
HALE	58	54	57	43	59	65
HALEY	52	50	64	38	52	61
HALSEY	37	38	(22)	(25)	(22)	55

KEY: Least - ○ Most - □ Masculine - ♂

	Success	Morality	Health	Warmth	Cheerful	Male - Female
HAMILTON	70	62	61	57	58	(78)♂
HANK	(22)	31	67	36	57	(86)♂
HANS	[77]	[76]	[72]	[72]	[71]	(78)♂
HARLEY	43	40	43	45	54	68
HARLOW	(23)	40	30	(23)	(15)	58
HAROLD	56	[75]	30	54	32	52
HARPER	62	41	45	37	42	69
HARRISON	[74]	58	[77]	64	58	(80)♂
HARRY	43	35	43	38	44	67
HARVEY	(24)	48	31	37	44	69
HASKEL	35	30	34	36	45	63
HAYDEN	61	50	60	55	53	(71)♂
HECTOR	(28)	(26)	45	(21)	(20)	(74)♂
HENRY	[72]	66	58	[79]	69	(74)♂
HERBERT	(29)	[76]	(15)	44	(28)	53
HERBY	(14)	42	(22)	31	52	59
HERMAN	47	[89]	(6)	41	(10)	59
HERSHEL	40	57	41	44	40	61
HEYWOOD	(17)	(17)	(25)	(18)	(26)	60

KEY: Least - ◯ Most - ☐ Masculine - ♂

	Success	Morality	Health	Warmth	Cheerful	Male - Female
HILARY	47	48	38	44	45	37
HIRAM	40	57	33	34	32	54
HOGAN	50	31	62	47	66	♂73
HOLDEN	69	64	62	54	48	70
HOLLIS	55	45	40	50	53	59
HOLMES	58	52	34	47	38	66
HOMER	41	□87	○6	48	○29	54
HORACE	36	65	○10	31	○7	66
HORTON	45	54	○26	44	38	68
HOUSTON	47	39	56	34	38	♂71
HOWARD	□74	□94	30	54	33	64
HOWIE	○15	○29	38	44	62	67
HUBERT	61	□79	○7	51	35	50
HUGH	□74	44	50	48	61	67
HUGO	○25	36	○24	○23	34	68
HUMPHREY	43	61	○18	38	○12	56
HUXLEY	50	40	32	36	44	60
HYATT	61	53	50	38	40	66
HYMIE	31	44	30	43	51	51

KEY: Least - ○ Most - □ Masculine - ♂

The Name Game

	Success	Morality	Health	Warmth	Cheerful	Male - Female
IAN	[91]	58	66	[72]	55	70
IGNAZIO	(20)	(18)	(21)	(15)	(21)	58
IGOR	(14)	(18)	(19)	(-5)	(5)	66
IKE	35	39	(27)	(16)	(25)	69
IRA	(27)	45	(28)	(19)	(24)	49
IRVING	65	[85]	(19)	65	38	53
IRWIN	42	59	(27)	36	40	56
ISAAC	69	[82]	49	66	32	(72)♂
IVAN	69	55	44	31	42	69
IVAR	47	43	30	30	(28)	62
JACK	54	(27)	[82]	44	[90]	(76)♂
JACKSON	54	47	52	51	53	(79)♂
JACOB	69	[100]	52	69	44	67
JACQUES	65	46	60	49	67	65
JAIME	48	42	62	62	66	56
JAKE	51	(20)	[85]	(29)	59	(84)♂
JAMES	[109]	[82]	[87]	[78]	[71]	(80)♂
JAMIE	49	49	58	55	63	56
JAN	58	34	56	40	54	54

KEY: Least - ( ) Most - [ ] Masculine - ♂

	Success	Morality	Health	Warmth	Cheerful	Male - Female
JARED	45	38	30	(24)	38	67
JARRETT	56	52	63	57	53	(73)♂
JARVIS	38	42	(28)	32	35	59
JASON	[79]	56	[80]	55	[83]	(76)♂
JASPER	48	45	47	57	60	55
JAVIER	34	(28)	56	39	40	70
JAY	52	42	64	44	49	(72)♂
JED	(22)	38	66	(29)	57	(77)♂
JEFF	70	33	[86]	44	[80]	(84)♂
JEFFERSON	65	62	[71]	54	60	(73)♂
JEFFREY	69	64	65	70	57	(74)♂
JEREMIAH	43	54	34	50	48	64
JEREMY	44	57	54	55	48	70
JEROME	34	37	65	31	63	(74)♂
JERRY	68	33	65	63	[83]	(75)♂
JESS	46	50	67	59	62	69
JESSIE	45	(16)	[74]	47	55	(71)♂
JETHRO	(10)	(27)	39	(15)	38	(72)♂
JIM	58	37	[90]	51	[71]	(80)♂

KEY: Least - ( ) Most - [ ] Masculine - ♂

	Success	Morality	Health	Warmth	Cheerful	Male - Female
JOACHIM	34	46	38	50	46	67
JOCK	(9)	(13)	56	(3)	35	83 ♂
JOE	45	41	67	54	63	77 ♂
JOEL	[76]	63	68	[76]	[74]	70
JOEY	(28)	41	57	58	63	64
JOHN	[86]	[72]	[95]	61	[73]	81 ♂
JONAH	61	[101]	46	[89]	42	64
JONAS	58	70	44	55	51	65
JONATHON	[89]	[82]	[74]	58	61	75 ♂
JORDAN	68	62	70	55	41	67
JOSE	(9)	(26)	39	35	57	72 ♂
JOSEPH	[82]	[89]	65	[89]	54	75 ♂
JOSH	60	54	[71]	[73]	70	77 ♂
JOSHUA	70	[101]	62	[81]	57	70
JUAN	(17)	(26)	31	(16)	(23)	67
JUDD	42	(23)	49	(20)	38	72 ♂
JULES	53	48	45	48	51	58
JULIAN	[71]	55	62	[76]	70	64
JULIUS	48	47	53	48	46	60

KEY: Least - ( ) Most - [ ] Masculine - ♂

	Success	Morality	Health	Warmth	Cheerful	Male - Female
JUSTIN	**79**	59	**80**	65	66	72
KANE	**77**	58	**72**	50	55	76
KAREEM	55	59	57	43	48	65
KARL	56	55	59	50	45	74
KEEGAN	49	39	45	42	45	59
KEENAN	54	47	54	38	50	69
KEITH	70	30	89	63	**88**	81
KELLY	56	53	**71**	62	67	53
KELSEY	60	55	**73**	60	63	58
KELVIN	**83**	66	62	51	42	70
KEN	62	45	**74**	43	61	75
KENDALL	**78**	56	68	46	**79**	65
KENNETH	**102**	**72**	**77**	**78**	63	76
KENT	**75**	70	**71**	49	60	75
KENTON	**71**	63	60	59	56	78
KERMIT	31	43	20	52	56	47
KEVIN	88	63	84	76	79	80
KIM	56	55	52	56	67	48
KIMBALL	65	62	58	56	57	66

KEY: Least - ○ Most - □ Masculine - ♂

The Name Game

	Success	Morality	Health	Warmth	Cheerful	Male - Female
KINCAID	62	45	41	33	37	67
KINGSLEY	53	57	59	57	48	68
KIRBY	51	56	55	41	59	66
KIRK	65	33	[80]	34	70	(80) ♂
KIT	38	50	50	43	61	50
KNUT	(29)	31	38	(13)	34	65
KURT	[77]	47	[87]	39	54	(86) ♂
KYLE	[77]	47	[89]	51	[74]	(82) ♂
LAIRD	54	53	44	37	30	59
LAMBERT	48	45	40	49	37	59
LAMONT	31	(29)	46	(24)	44	65
LANCE	59	45	61	48	52	(71) ♂
LANDON	66	57	66	55	57	69
LANE	52	37	53	38	43	64
LANGDON	56	60	47	34	36	61
LANGLEY	[92]	[76]	42	52	50	56
LANNY	38	36	41	58	63	50
LARRY	40	39	43	(29)	41	67
LARS	53	39	61	40	37	(71) ♂

KEY: Least - ( ) Most - [ ] Masculine - ♂

The Name Game

	Success	Morality	Health	Warmth	Cheerful	Male - Female
LASZLO	30	(25)	(28)	31	(21)	65
LAWRENCE	[82]	66	53	55	48	65
LAWTON	60	65	48	38	37	70
LEE	[77]	36	[74]	47	58	(71)♂
LEIF	(27)	37	56	37	53	64
LEIGHTON	61	53	55	54	41	66
LELAND	45	58	45	57	51	59
LEO	44	33	63	55	63	(78)♂
LEON	(22)	30	39	(17)	(29)	69
LEONARD	[72]	[75]	36	55	37	67
LEOPOLD	45	51	(26)	32	(29)	60
LEROY	(17)	(25)	40	37	39	(75)♂
LES	41	42	41	46	50	59
LESLIE	41	57	54	57	55	49
LESTER	44	52	(11)	48	(11)	49
LEVI	35	44	35	39	(29)	67
LEWIS	70	65	54	49	54	(72)♂
LINCOLN	[86]	[97]	45	[73]	(20)	69
LINDSAY	[75]	58	63	63	57	49

KEY: Least - ( ) Most - [ ] Masculine - ♂

The Name Game

	Success	Morality	Health	Warmth	Cheerful	Male - Female
LINK	35	30	30	31	34	65
LINUS	38	69	37	67	56	56
LIONEL	42	32	33	32	48	67
LIVINGSTON	67	66	39	45	39	62
LLOYD	□ 77	66	55	44	45	♂ 75
LOGAN	□ 76	42	64	46	46	♂ 74
LORENZO	49	○ 24	□ 83	46	54	♂ 85
LOUIE	○ 24	○ 17	31	○ 29	47	♂ 71
LOUIS	51	54	42	59	53	63
LUCAS	54	45	49	49	49	70
LUCIAN	53	46	51	42	39	57
LUDLOW	41	45	○ 21	40	○ 27	64
LUDWIG	54	62	○ 25	37	31	66
LUKE	45	52	62	43	43	♂ 78
LUTHER	39	38	38	○ 21	○ 29	70
LYLE	46	33	46	39	42	63
LYNDON	62	55	65	59	52	68
LYNN	45	62	50	50	43	42
MAC	30	○ 25	39	○ 28	45	♂ 81

KEY: Least - ○ Most - □ Masculine - ♂

	Success	Morality	Health	Warmth	Cheerful	Male - Female
MACKENZIE	71 □	58	53	55	62	56
MACNAIR	62	60	49	44	39	66
MADISON	106 □	87 □	70	61	55	72 ♂
MALCOLM	74 □	45	56	34	36	79 ♂
MALLORY	54	49	46	56	54	45
MANDEL	46	33	26 ○	42	48	54
MANFRED	28 ○	26 ○	34	23 ○	25 ○	71 ♂
MANNY	39	29 ○	37	32	58	61
MANUEL	23 ○	51	42	42	42	75 ♂
MARCEL	49	40	45	45	55	50
MARCELO	45	29 ○	38	40	46	67
MARCOS	39	26 ○	41	21 ○	28 ○	65
MARCUS	61	49	86 □	65	79 □	81 ♂
MARIO	46	45	55	49	58	81 ♂
MARK	92 □	35	95 □	48	76 □	83 ♂
MARLON	59	65	43	62	52	66
MARLOW	57	54	54	44	54	64
MARSHALL	66	68	66	57	53	70
MARTIN	75 □	61	45	44	48	65

KEY: Least - ○ Most - □ Masculine - ♂

	Success	Morality	Health	Warmth	Cheerful	Male - Female
MARTY	39	(29)	37	32	51	63
MARVIN	(24)	37	(29)	38	31	64
MASON	62	45	48	(29)	42	68
MATT	[77]	53	[81]	61	67	(82) ♂
MATTHEW	[79]	66	[82]	55	[71]	(78) ♂
MAURICE	62	52	31	62	41	61
MAX	69	43	[71]	37	52	(82) ♂
MAXIMILIAN	[77]	50	60	48	51	(79) ♂
MAXWELL	[72]	57	53	49	49	68
MAYNARD	32	39	(28)	(27)	35	58
MEAD	38	44	50	41	37	48
MEL	38	(19)	36	(21)	(27)	62
MELBOURNE	52	63	43	53	50	67
MELVILLE	51	65	35	53	(28)	60
MELVIN	(13)	31	(0)	(25)	(11)	43
MEREDITH	58	54	53	62	55	50
MERLE	(19)	40	(22)	45	45	56
MERRICK	58	49	49	57	52	(71) ♂
MERRILL	63	58	57	66	63	62

KEY: Least - ○ Most - □ Masculine - ♂

	Success	Morality	Health	Warmth	Cheerful	Male - Female
MERVIN	30	65	35	37	34	55
MICHAEL	70	42	82 □	62	95 □	83 ♂
MICKEY	28 ○	22 ○	52	38	73 □	54
MIKE	73 □	55	71 □	56	71 □	81 ♂
MILES	58	54	55	46	57	67
MILO	37	29 ○	33	20 ○	51	63
MILTON	78 □	85 □	31	54	38	69
MISCHA	48	56	72 □	61	64	56
MITCH	60	46	78 □	47	59	75 ♂
MITCHELL	78 □	40	78 □	50	72 □	77 ♂
MONROE	47	69	46	69	76 □	57
MONTGOMERY	68	53	58	46	36	68
MONTY	51	35	41	38	51	65
MORDECAI	28 ○	43	24 ○	31	21 ○	55
MOREY	33	31	25 ○	26 ○	26 ○	56
MORGAN	63	52	55	44	59	63
MORLEY	46	52	32	40	45	61
MORRIS	55	49	50	58	54	62
MORT	37	48	31	35	39	72 ♂

KEY: Least - ○ Most - □ Masculine - ♂

	Success	Morality	Health	Warmth	Cheerful	Male - Female
MORTIMER	(28)	54	(9)	36	(11)	54
MORTON	47	59	34	44	48	66
MOSES	62	[121]	44	[92]	(24)	(78) ♂
MOSS	38	46	42	42	33	54
MUHAMMED	57	[87]	(13)	(17)	(-14)	(78) ♂
MURDOCK	49	44	38	33	45	(71) ♂
MURRAY	45	54	38	51	56	64
MURRY	(28)	32	36	(25)	34	65
MYRON	39	43	34	36	30	52
NATE	47	49	55	52	64	67
NATHAN	[83]	[89]	49	59	49	69
NATHANIEL	59	65	66	70	54	(72) ♂
NEAL	59	52	54	54	54	(75) ♂
NED	(27)	39	46	45	49	65
NEIL	[82]	38	[81]	61	57	(79) ♂
NELSON	59	59	52	41	39	(76) ♂
NESTOR	(24)	34	(20)	33	34	48
NEVILLE	52	48	43	43	46	56
NEWTON	59	39	43	(23)	32	62

KEY: Least - ○ Most - □ Masculine - ♂

The Name Game

	Success	Morality	Health	Warmth	Cheerful	Male - Female
NICHOLAS	[84]	59	[79]	61	58	(78)♂
NICK	48	49	61	47	[73]	(77)♂
NIELS	56	63	[71]	60	52	69
NIGEL	62	58	49	58	38	69
NOEL	60	[71]	52	63	55	45
NOLAN	51	57	48	50	50	68
NOLL	33	42	43	(21)	(25)	59
NORMAN	62	[75]	(20)	62	(19)	55
NORRIS	47	46	46	40	32	64
NORTHROP	54	61	45	55	44	67
NORTON	[75]	[73]	30	38	(27)	57
NOUBERT	(29)	34	(17)	(20)	(20)	54
OGDEN	40	33	(28)	(16)	32	61
OLAF	(28)	48	(27)	38	(29)	64
OLIVER	[72]	67	38	52	34	65
OLLIE	(22)	(28)	34	46	45	60
OMAR	69	69	38	(11)	(10)	(74)♂
ORSON	[79]	[80]	(22)	41	(8)	62
ORVILLE	67	[93]	(-6)	55	(23)	47

KEY: Least - ○ Most - □ Masculine - ♂

The Name Game

	Success	Morality	Health	Warmth	Cheerful	Male - Female
OSBORN	51	41	34	36	49	68
OSCAR	36	37	(26)	39	61	65
OSGOOD	45	52	(22)	30	30	56
OSMOND	36	53	37	36	40	56
OSWALD	40	39	(24)	(29)	34	60
OTIS	(15)	52	40	34	33	64
OTTO	36	33	42	(26)	47	(71) ♂
OWEN	52	46	50	32	33	(72) ♂
OZZIE	(29)	(29)	(27)	36	53	59
PABLO	(27)	45	39	42	44	(76) ♂
PACO	(11)	30	(28)	(11)	36	67
PADDY	(27)	54	47	58	58	53
PALLADIN	36	45	35	43	31	57
PALMER	[84]	42	56	38	32	70
PARKER	[99]	64	[82]	56	47	(79) ♂
PARNELL	48	52	33	42	39	56
PARRISH	50	44	44	41	38	65
PASCAL	55	43	40	42	49	61
PAT	51	55	50	54	62	59

KEY: Least - ( ) Most - [ ] Masculine - ♂

The Name Game

	Success	Morality	Health	Warmth	Cheerful	Male - Female
PATRICK	70	58	[79]	55	69	(77)♂
PATTON	63	59	58	43	50	69
PAUL	[71]	63	[80]	62	69	(78)♂
PAXTON	65	51	40	31	35	69
PEDRO	31	44	41	39	50	70
PENN	49	47	48	55	49	66
PENROD	44	50	(29)	31	34	50
PERCIVAL	40	59	(29)	(27)	(20)	53
PERCY	32	60	(27)	45	41	43
PERRY	49	48	50	61	52	69
PETE	55	53	59	50	61	(76)♂
PETER	[91]	[76]	[73]	[73]	65	(73)♂
PHIL	51	57	53	37	48	(75)♂
PHILLIP	[84]	45	[73]	44	37	(75)♂
PHINEAS	38	60	(29)	(25)	(25)	54
PIERCE	[75]	35	66	32	37	64
PIERRE	55	32	44	44	52	68
PONCE	37	37	35	33	42	62
PRENTICE	[72]	65	36	46	31	41

KEY: Least - ○ Most - □ Masculine - ♂

The Name Game

	Success	Morality	Health	Warmth	Cheerful	Male - Female
PRESCOTT	69	60	55	51	54	69
PRESTON	64	57	57	57	58	72 ♂
PURVIS	36	49	21 (least)	45	38	49
QUENTIN	54	40	44	25 (least)	33	65
QUINCY	63	54	47	50	51	59
QUINN	64	56	60	53	57	66
RADCLIFFE	65	56	50	43	45	72 ♂
RAFAEL	55	59	51	51	49	71 ♂
RALEIGH	54	49	51	45	40	65
RALPH	30	23 (least)	34	32	65	68
RAMIN	41	36	36	26 (least)	37	63
RAMON	30	34	30	13 (least)	26 (least)	67
RAMSEY	54	48	52	52	50	71 ♂
RAND	61	41	55	42	49	71 ♂
RANDALL	70	53	60	33	38	73 ♂
RANDOLPH	76 (most)	73 (most)	50	58	37	64
RANDY	44	24 (least)	83 (most)	49	84 (most)	72 ♂
RAPHAEL	47	53	45	51	53	63
RAUL	36	42	37	29 (least)	40	68

KEY: Least - ○ Most - □ Masculine - ♂

The Name Game

	Success	Morality	Health	Warmth	Cheerful	Male - Female
RAY	64	○26	□73	45	53	♂71
RAYBURN	47	50	44	36	38	♂72
RAYMOND	□72	55	66	58	55	♂75
REDFORD	65	53	66	49	52	♂76
REGGIE	34	36	60	52	□73	♂71
REGINALD	□72	□81	51	46	○26	62
REMINGTON	□85	63	70	50	50	♂76
REUBEN	35	41	40	○29	○20	68
REX	64	○13	66	○14	48	♂87
REYNOLD	58	50	50	43	42	♂71
RHETT	57	39	54	47	49	♂72
RICH	67	49	65	59	64	♂76
RICHARD	□74	55	□80	59	66	♂77
RICHIE	33	52	50	53	68	64
RICHMOND	□74	58	61	54	57	♂72
RICK	69	○13	□98	○28	□80	♂81
RIF	47	34	43	○21	○20	53
RILEY	38	○29	50	○29	47	64
RIP	○26	○7	36	○2	37	59

KEY: Least - ○ Most - □ Masculine - ♂

The Name Game

	Success	Morality	Health	Warmth	Cheerful	Male - Female
ROB	68	50	[85]	59	68	♂ 81
ROBERT	[91]	[72]	[89]	[75]	[76]	♂ 86
ROBIN	58	61	59	69	58	57
ROBINSON	56	66	70	54	60	66
ROCKY	(23)	(25)	62	(25)	46	♂ 86
ROD	44	30	54	(29)	54	♂ 76
RODDY	36	36	43	34	60	66
RODERICK	61	57	53	32	40	♂ 73
RODNEY	47	42	52	52	59	66
ROGER	69	44	[71]	55	54	♂ 77
ROLAND	61	51	49	59	65	♂ 71
ROMAN	47	51	55	35	42	♂ 74
RON	50	31	55	54	53	♂ 76
RONALD	[83]	[73]	46	38	40	65
RONNIE	36	40	53	37	64	63
RORY	43	45	49	43	53	60
ROSCOE	(13)	(9)	44	(27)	55	♂ 78
ROSS	[99]	56	[88]	66	[82]	♂ 80
ROY	43	55	60	48	53	♂ 79

KEY: Least - ( ) Most - [ ] Masculine - ♂

The Name Game

	Success	Morality	Health	Warmth	Cheerful	Male - Female
RUDOLPH	52	61	44	56	48	63
RUDY	32	50	46	52	65	60
RUDYARD	50	52	41	38	49	64
RUFUS	○2	○12	○27	○20	○23	67
RUPERT	34	62	○12	39	○12	53
RUSS	54	58	66	63	66	♂74
RUSSEL	64	62	62	63	49	♂74
RUSTY	39	54	61	57	59	63
RUTLEDGE	61	54	53	45	48	♂72
RYAN	□76	35	□80	46	□74	♂76
SAL	○16	○14	○26	○14	33	67
SALVADOR	35	58	47	35	○16	♂79
SAM	47	42	59	44	67	♂72
SAMSON	52	50	63	42	45	♂75
SAMUEL	58	□94	34	61	31	68
SANDERS	52	58	52	53	49	70
SANDY	42	43	56	62	70	59
SANFORD	46	44	43	42	46	65
SAUL	41	38	31	○15	○12	68

KEY: Least - ○ Most - □ Masculine - ♂

	Success	Morality	Health	Warmth	Cheerful	Male - Female
SCOTT	[90]	40	[91]	62	[101]	(82) ♂
SEAN	58	37	[85]	48	[73]	(77) ♂
SEBASTIAN	[75]	[72]	46	[79]	57	67
SELBY	55	55	40	41	37	52
SERGE	42	52	52	58	61	(71) ♂
SERGIO	32	(22)	36	36	44	64
SETH	55	48	45	43	59	63
SEYMOUR	48	70	(5)	53	(23)	44
SHANE	63	45	[72]	38	48	(79) ♂
SHANNON	37	40	52	49	57	46
SHAWN	49	49	63	68	55	58
SHEA	52	62	49	46	52	55
SHELBY	59	63	47	60	54	55
SHELDON	[74]	68	35	55	38	56
SHELLEY	47	56	51	50	55	49
SHERIDAN	53	62	50	45	45	67
SHERLOCK	59	50	41	37	51	64
SHERMAN	53	47	33	32	43	63
SHERWIN	48	56	35	42	45	55

KEY: Least - ○ Most - □ Masculine - ♂

	Success	Morality	Health	Warmth	Cheerful	Male - Female
SID	(23)	(15)	36	(24)	38	66
SIDNEY	59	69	34	[78]	69	56
SIEGFRIED	63	49	37	40	40	67
SIGMUND	60	62	(11)	36	(24)	63
SILVESTER	46	42	39	38	40	69
SIMON	[71]	65	40	46	44	59
SINCLAIR	68	63	47	52	52	67
SKIPP	(15)	(28)	50	33	64	63
SLOAN	46	53	54	41	54	65
SOLOMON	70	[108]	(29)	56	(19)	68
SOMERSET	34	43	43	42	32	54
SONNY	(29)	41	45	38	52	61
SPENCER	[92]	66	[73]	55	58	♂(72)
STACY	46	43	51	54	58	51
STAN	49	39	50	45	58	66
STANFORD	[78]	61	59	43	44	♂(71)
STANLEY	58	[76]	(21)	49	(23)	60
STANTON	65	57	48	41	43	66
STEPHEN	[71]	69	[74]	61	68	♂(74)

KEY: Least - ( ) Most - [ ] Masculine - ♂

	Success	Morality	Health	Warmth	Cheerful	Male - Female
STERLING	68	59	65	47	58	67
STEVE	68	47	68	47	55	(77)♂
STEVEN	[93]	62	[95]	[88]	[79]	(84)♂
STEWART	64	59	61	58	63	68
STUART	[77]	62	58	39	42	65
SVEN	51	70	67	59	60	(79)♂
SYLVESTER	54	49	43	49	58	67
TAB	(27)	(27)	52	(28)	58	64
TAD	61	(7)	[85]	39	65	(80)♂
TANNER	48	38	55	42	50	70
TED	68	(27)	[73]	54	58	67
TERENCE	65	54	42	41	45	63
TERRY	55	46	61	53	[75]	56
THAYER	54	51	46	(25)	36	63
THEO	45	59	58	57	59	65
THEODORE	[83]	[92]	48	[76]	33	(73)♂
THOMAS	[102]	[76]	[78]	69	58	(81)♂
THOR	41	48	53	(28)	(27)	(86)♂
THORNTON	57	37	33	(6)	(22)	66

KEY: Least - ○ Most - □ Masculine - ♂

The Name Game

	Success	Morality	Health	Warmth	Cheerful	Male - Female
THURSTON	64	54	43	48	48	68
TIM	47	49	58	50	62	♂71
TIMOTHY	□79	55	66	69	□80	69
TITUS	38	43	50	41	37	♂72
TOBIAS	52	66	52	47	42	63
TOBY	31	39	44	34	55	62
TODD	□76	○23	□89	42	□78	♂80
TOM	□72	42	□83	46	□73	♂76
TONY	□72	37	□91	56	□88	♂82
TORRANCE	49	58	43	43	44	63
TRACY	48	55	65	54	□72	56
TRAVIS	□72	49	61	52	57	70
TREBOR	58	57	52	49	53	66
TRENT	□89	34	□85	39	53	♂80
TREVOR	□77	38	□72	36	59	♂77
TRISTAN	55	58	59	50	59	60
TROY	67	35	□95	52	66	♂82
TUCKER	44	55	58	46	61	68
TULLY	○22	○25	30	○14	33	55

KEY: Least - ○ Most - □ Masculine - ♂

Name	Success	Morality	Health	Warmth	Cheerful	Male - Female
TY	49	53	61	58	62	66
TYLER	63	57	61	41	54	75 ○♂
TYNAN	42	58	51	50	45	69
TYRONE	14 ○	0 ○	80 □	22 ○	24 ○	83 ○♂
TYSON	45	46	48	21 ○	43	72 ○♂
ULRIC	35	47	27 ○	33	32	58
ULYSSES	89 □	80 □	55	35	21 ○	75 ○♂
VAN	49	52	65	48	55	70
VANCE	49	52	70	57	57	65
VASSILY	30	46	42	50	50	55
VAUGHN	52	54	55	56	52	67
VERN	24 ○	54	30	45	52	63
VERNON	49	62	18 ○	44	45	61
VICTOR	63	40	58	38	38	79 ○♂
VINCE	46	27 ○	58	28 ○	45	74 ○♂
VINCENT	79 □	61	67	51	57	75 ○♂
VINNY	25 ○	38	64	47	58	68
VIRGIL	63	79 □	34	48	27 ○	49
VITO	23 ○	19 ○	39	16 ○	25 ○	75 ○♂

KEY: Least - ○ Most - □ Masculine - ♂

The Name Game

	Success	Morality	Health	Warmth	Cheerful	Male - Female
VLADIMIR	□ 84	□ 79	○ 26	○ 14	○ 12	♂ 72
WADE	54	38	56	44	56	♂ 71
WALDO	○ 21	41	○ -3	34	○ 4	44
WALLACE	□ 77	□ 87	37	62	45	61
WALLY	○ 28	46	○ 28	33	52	64
WALT	48	63	62	53	55	69
WALTER	□ 82	□ 77	○ 29	69	36	64
WALTON	51	63	55	68	51	♂ 74
WARD	49	69	60	59	58	♂ 75
WARNER	66	69	64	63	□ 73	♂ 74
WARREN	□ 75	53	60	43	35	♂ 71
WARTON	36	40	○ 27	○ 13	○ 9	64
WAYNE	38	44	46	35	41	♂ 73
WENDELL	□ 71	□ 77	37	61	44	55
WERNER	61	59	55	51	53	♂ 71
WES	54	50	69	61	62	64
WESLEY	64	58	64	68	53	63
WESTON	70	62	68	56	57	66
WHITNEY	57	46	47	59	50	50

KEY: Least - ○ Most - □ Masculine - ♂

The Name Game

	Success	Morality	Health	Warmth	Cheerful	Male - Female
WILBUR	(17)	50	(20)	(19)	(20)	58
WILEY	44	50	43	42	53	69
WILFRED	40	50	33	(18)	(12)	61
WILL	52	61	64	61	56	(72) ♂
WILLARD	48	54	45	46	48	(71) ♂
WILLIAM	[81]	[85]	60	41	(29)	(74) ♂
WILMER	(23)	34	(22)	(20)	(13)	55
WILTON	51	60	46	43	45	69
WINFIELD	65	60	43	49	50	68
WINSLOW	54	45	31	(21)	(17)	59
WINSTON	[81]	62	40	(21)	(7)	65
WINTHROP	61	60	50	40	52	68
WOLFGANG	59	59	32	38	40	70
WOODROW	60	[73]	55	62	54	69
WOODY	43	54	70	56	[72]	66
WYATT	49	42	41	(22)	33	68
WYLIE	(17)	(29)	(24)	31	42	59
XAVIER	[75]	42	57	39	38	68
YANCY	(29)	38	33	57	55	47

KEY: Least - ○ Most - □ Masculine - ♂

The Name Game

	Success	Morality	Health	Warmth	Cheerful	Male - Female
YURI	48	54	55	42	50	64
ZACHARY	49	51	57	41	45	69
ZANE	37	56	55	40	47	65
ZEKE	31	(24)	37	(17)	31	(73)♂

KEY: Least - ○ Most - □ Masculine - ♂

Chapter Five

Male Names that Imply Success

The following list includes boys' names which people identify with success, ambition, intelligence and creativity:

JAMES	109
MADISON	106
CHARLES	105
ALEXANDER	102
KENNETH	102
THOMAS	102
PARKER	99
ROSS	99
ADAM	93
COLBY	93
STEVEN	93
DAVID	92
DREW	92
EDWARD	92
LANGLEY	92
MARK	92
SPENCER	92
IAN	91
PETER	91
ROBERT	91
BRAD	90
SCOTT	90
ANDREW	89
BENJAMIN	89
COLLIN	89
CONRAD	89
JONATHON	89
TRENT	89
ULYSSES	89
BARTHOLEMEW	88
CHRISTOPHER	88
KEVIN	88
ELLIOT	86
JOHN	86
LINCOLN	86
ABRAHAM	85
GREGORY	85
REMINGTON	85
ADOLPH	84
ALAN	84
DOUGLAS	84
NICHOLAS	84
PALMER	84
PHILLIP	84
VLADIMIR	84
GEOFFREY	83
KELVIN	83
NATHAN	83
RONALD	83
THEODORE	83
BLAKE	82
JOSEPH	82
LAWRENCE	82
NEIL	82

WALTER	82	STUART	77
CARTER	81	TREVOR	77
CHAD	81	WALLACE	77
CLARK	81	ADDISON	76
DONALD	81	BOB	76
WILLIAM	81	CALVIN	76
WINSTON	81	CHANDLER	76
ALDEN	79	CRAIG	76
BASIL	79	JOEL	76
BRADEN	79	LOGAN	76
EDMUND	79	RANDOLPH	76
FRANKLIN	79	RYAN	76
JASON	79	TODD	76
JUSTIN	79	ARTHUR	75
MATTHEW	79	BRENTON	75
ORSON	79	KENT	75
TIMOTHY	79	LINDSAY	75
VINCENT	79	MARTIN	75
BRANDON	78	NORTON	75
GRANT	78	PIERCE	75
KENDALL	78	SEBASTIAN	75
MILTON	78	WARREN	75
MITCHELL	78	XAVIER	75
STANFORD	78	BEN	74
BRADFORD	77	DANIEL	74
DRAKE	77	FRANK	74
DUSTIN	77	HARRISON	74
GRAHAM	77	HOWARD	74
HANS	77	HUGH	74
KANE	77	MALCOLM	74
KURT	77	RICHARD	74
KYLE	77	RICHMOND	74
LEE	77	SHELDON	74
LLOYD	77	ASHFORD	73
MATT	77	BOND	73
MAXIMILIAN	77	BRENDAN	73

Chapter Six

Male Names that Suggest Morality

The table in this chapter lists male names in order of perceived "morality." Morality includes the following important and interrelated components: obedience, respectfulness, religiousness, loyalty and trustworthiness.

MOSES	121	WILLIAM	85
SOLOMON	108	MILTON	85
ABRAHAM	106	IRVING	85
JOSHUA	101	FRANKLIN	84
JONAH	101	JAMES	82
JACOB	100	EDWARD	82
ABEL	99	JONATHON	82
LINCOLN	97	CLARK	82
HOWARD	94	ISAAC	82
SAMUEL	94	FILBERT	82
BARTHOLEMEW	93	REGINALD	81
ERNEST	93	AMORY	81
ORVILLE	93	ULYSSES	80
ALFRED	93	ORSON	80
THEODORE	92	CHARLES	79
ELMER	90	VLADIMIR	79
NATHAN	89	GRAHAM	79
JOSEPH	89	BEN	79
HERMAN	89	GABRIEL	79
MADISON	87	VIRGIL	79
WALLACE	87	HUBERT	79
MUHAMMED	87	EDWIN	78
HOMER	87	FRANCIS	78
ELLIOT	86	WALTER	77
ARCHIBALD	86	WENDELL	77

THOMAS	76	SEYMOUR	70
LANGLEY	76	EZRA	70
PETER	76	GAVIN	69
HANS	76	STEPHEN	69
STANLEY	76	OMAR	69
HERBERT	76	WARNER	69
EDMUND	75	SIDNEY	69
LEONARD	75	WARD	69
EUGENE	75	MONROE	69
NORMAN	75	LINUS	69
HAROLD	75	SHELDON	68
BENJAMIN	74	MARSHALL	68
CHRISTIAN	74	OLIVER	67
RONALD	73	FITZPATRICK	67
CARTER	73	CYRUS	67
RANDOLPH	73	DREW	66
NORTON	73	SPENCER	66
CHESTER	73	KELVIN	66
WOODROW	73	LAWRENCE	66
BERNARD	73	DONALD	66
AMOS	73	MATTHEW	66
KENNETH	72	BRADFORD	66
ROBERT	72	LLOYD	66
JOHN	72	DANIEL	66
BASIL	72	HENRY	66
SEBASTIAN	72	FITZGERALD	66
FLOYD	72	ANTHONY	66
CORNELIUS	72	LIVINGSTON	66
ANDREW	71	ANSEL	66
GREGORY	71	GRAYSON	66
GEOFFREY	71	ROBINSON	66
BRIGHAM	71	TOBIAS	66
NOEL	71	ALEXANDER	65
KENT	70	PRENTICE	65
JONAS	70	SIMON	65
SVEN	70	LEWIS	65

Chapter Seven

Male Names that Connote Health

"Healthy," in terms of our findings, consists of the following important and interrelated qualities: popularity, athleticism, appearance, confidence and assertiveness. As defined here, "healthy" identifies a distinctive and appealing quality which some parents may very much like to see become part of their child's image.

CHAD	98	CHUCK	86
RICK	98	JEFF	86
JOHN	95	BLAKE	86
STEVEN	95	BRIAN	85
MARK	95	DAVID	85
TROY	95	ROB	85
BUCK	95	COLLIN	85
CRAIG	94	DRAKE	85
BRAD	91	SEAN	85
SCOTT	91	TRENT	85
TONY	91	DUKE	85
JIM	90	DEREK	85
ROBERT	89	JAKE	85
GREGORY	89	DAMON	85
DREW	89	TAD	85
KYLE	89	KEVIN	84
KEITH	89	COLBY	84
TODD	89	TOM	83
ERIC	89	GARY	83
ROSS	88	LORENZO	83
JAMES	87	RANDY	83
KURT	87	MATTHEW	82
MARCUS	86	PARKER	82

MICHAEL	82	LEE	74
JACK	82	JESSIE	74
CURTIS	82	ANDRE	74
MATT	81	PETER	73
NEIL	81	SPENCER	73
CHRISTOPHER	80	DANIEL	73
PAUL	80	CHANDLER	73
JUSTIN	80	COLTON	73
JASON	80	KELSEY	73
RICHARD	80	BRENT	73
DEAN	80	PHILLIP	73
CLAY	80	BJORN	73
BILL	80	TED	73
RYAN	80	RAY	73
KIRK	80	HANS	72
TYRONE	80	KANE	72
NICHOLAS	79	MISCHA	72
PATRICK	79	BRICE	72
BRUCE	79	BEAU	72
THOMAS	78	SHANE	72
GRANT	78	TREVOR	72
MITCH	78	FRANK	72
MITCHELL	78	AUSTIN	72
KENNETH	77	KENT	71
HARRISON	77	NIELS	71
BRANDON	77	JEFFERSON	71
DARREN	77	CALVIN	71
BOB	76	MIKE	71
GLEN	76	JOSH	71
GUY	76	KELLY	71
DAN	76	CLINT	71
JONATHON	74	ROGER	71
STEPHEN	74	MAX	71
CARY	74	FABIAN	71
DERRICK	74	DARREL	71
KEN	74	MADISON	70

Chapter Eight

Male Names that Suggest Warmth

The name characteristic "warm,"as used here, includes the following important and interrelated qualities: loving, caring, kind and generous. This is a distinctive and appealing quality which someone may very much like to see become a part of his image or the image of a son. It is interesting to note that boys' names, in general, do not rate very high on the warmth scale.

MOSES	92	LINCOLN	73
JOSEPH	89	AMORY	73
JONAH	89	DAVID	72
STEVEN	88	HANS	72
JOSHUA	81	IAN	72
FRANCIS	81	CHRISTIAN	72
HENRY	79	ALAN	72
ANSON	79	BEN	71
SEBASTIAN	79	NATHANIEL	70
JAMES	78	JEFFREY	70
KENNETH	78	BRIAN	69
SIDNEY	78	THOMAS	69
KEVIN	76	GLEN	69
JOEL	76	CHARLES	69
JULIAN	76	TIMOTHY	69
GABRIEL	76	ROBIN	69
THEODORE	76	JACOB	69
ROBERT	75	MONROE	69
BOB	73	WALTER	69
PETER	73	DREW	68
DANIEL	73	WESLEY	68
JOSH	73	SHAWN	68

WALTON	68	PAUL	62
DUNCAN	68	KELLY	62
LINUS	67	ANTONIO	62
ROSS	66	JAIME	62
GEOFFREY	66	SANDY	62
MERRILL	66	WOODROW	62
GRAHAM	66	MEREDITH	62
ISAAC	66	DARBY	62
ALBERT	66	MARLON	62
MARCUS	65	WALLACE	62
JUSTIN	65	MAURICE	62
CARY	65	NORMAN	62
DENNIS	65	JOHN	61
BARRY	65	ERIC	61
IRVING	65	GARY	61
ELMER	65	MATT	61
HARRISON	64	NEIL	61
BRANDON	64	NICHOLAS	61
DANA	64	STEPHEN	61
KEITH	63	MISCHA	61
EDWARD	63	MADISON	61
RUSS	63	BRADLEY	61
JERRY	63	WES	61
EDDIE	63	AARON	61
WARNER	63	ANTHONY	61
DOUGLAS	63	GIOVANNI	61
LINDSAY	63	WILL	61
RUSSEL	63	GARETH	61
ASHLEY	63	ASHBY	61
ANGELO	63	FARRELL	61
DELANEY	63	CLARK	61
NOEL	63	PERRY	61
GIUSEPPE	63	WENDELL	61
ABRAHAM	63	SAMUEL	61
SCOTT	62	AMOS	61
MICHAEL	62	FRED	61

Chapter Nine

Male Names that Imply Cheerfulness

"Cheerful," as defined in my rating system, encompasses the following important and interrelated qualities: playful, friendly, curious and humorous.

SCOTT	101	MONROE	76
MICHAEL	95	MARK	76
ERIC	95	TERRY	75
GARY	93	CHUCK	75
CHARLIE	91	JOEL	74
EDDIE	90	GREG	74
JACK	90	GREGORY	74
KEITH	88	KYLE	74
TONY	88	BILLY	74
RANDY	84	RYAN	74
DANIEL	83	DAVID	73
JERRY	83	DREW	73
JASON	83	WARNER	73
ROSS	82	JOHN	73
BRIAN	80	REGGIE	73
TIMOTHY	80	SEAN	73
DENNIS	80	NICK	73
CASEY	80	TOM	73
JEFF	80	GUS	73
RICK	80	MICKEY	73
STEVEN	79	WOODY	72
KEVIN	79	DENNY	72
MARCUS	79	DERRICK	72
CHAD	79	TRACY	72
KENDALL	79	MITCHELL	72
TODD	78	JAMES	71
ROBERT	76	HANS	71

MIKE	71	JAIME	66
ARTIE	71	DARBY	66
MATTHEW	71	RICHARD	66
DONALD	71	ANDY	66
DAVY	71	DON	66
JIM	71	CODY	66
JULIAN	70	TROY	66
JOSH	70	HOGAN	66
DUNCAN	70	DEREK	66
BARRY	70	PETER	65
SANDY	70	GEOFFREY	65
DARREL	70	BRADLEY	65
KIRK	70	ROLAND	65
HENRY	69	CALVIN	65
SIDNEY	69	BILL	65
DANA	69	COURTNEY	65
PAUL	69	RUDY	65
DONOVAN	69	ALEC	65
CORY	69	BRAD	65
PATRICK	69	DARREN	65
CHIP	69	AL	65
STEPHEN	68	CRAIG	65
ROB	68	TAD	65
RICHIE	68	RALPH	65
DAVE	68	MISCHA	64
BEN	67	RICH	64
GLEN	67	NATE	64
KELLY	67	FRITZ	64
MATT	67	RONNIE	64
KIM	67	SKIPP	64
JACQUES	67	KENNETH	63
SAM	67	BOB	63
JUSTIN	66	MERRILL	63
CARY	66	BRANDON	63
RUSS	66	KELSEY	63
GIUSEPPE	66	STEWART	63

Chapter Ten

Male Names that Connote Masculinity

Names with high or low qualities of masculinity or femininity may be of central concern to some who are in the process of selecting a name.

CONAN	94	KYLE	82
BUCK	91	MATT	82
DUKE	89	TROY	82
REX	87	BRUCE	82
CHAD	86	MAX	82
ROBERT	86	ABDUL	82
BILL	86	DAMON	82
HANK	86	BORG	82
KURT	86	BRUNO	82
ROCKY	86	KEITH	81
THOR	86	RICK	81
LORENZO	85	MARCUS	81
ERIC	84	DAVID	81
JEFF	84	JOHN	81
STEVEN	84	MIKE	81
GREGORY	84	ROB	81
JAKE	84	DEREK	81
BUTCH	84	CRAIG	81
MICHAEL	83	BOB	81
MARK	83	THOMAS	81
CHUCK	83	MARIO	81
JOCK	83	FLINT	81
TYRONE	83	MAC	81
SCOTT	82	DRAKE	81
TONY	82	ROSS	80

Name	Score
KEVIN	80
TODD	80
JAMES	80
JIM	80
KIRK	80
TAD	80
HARRISON	80
GRANT	80
TRENT	80
COLBY	80
DEAN	80
CLINT	80
BRONSON	80
GARY	79
BRIAN	79
BRAD	79
SVEN	79
NEIL	79
GARRICK	79
BRADSHAW	79
DILLON	79
JACKSON	79
ROY	79
MAXIMILIAN	79
BUD	79
SHANE	79
BLAKE	79
PARKER	79
VICTOR	79
MALCOLM	79
SALVADOR	79
GREG	78
DERRICK	78
HANS	78
MATTHEW	78
DARREL	78
PAUL	78
LEO	78
COLLIN	78
NICHOLAS	78
HAMILTON	78
KENTON	78
CHARLES	78
BAXTER	78
ROSCOE	78
FRANK	78
BRADFORD	78
BURKE	78
LUKE	78
BART	78
DALLAS	78
MOSES	78
MUHAMMED	78
SEAN	77
NICK	77
MITCHELL	77
JOSH	77
PATRICK	77
GLEN	77
RICHARD	77
DARREN	77
JOE	77
TREVOR	77
ANTHONY	77
GINO	77
JED	77
STEVE	77
ROGER	77
CLIFF	77
ABE	77
COLTON	77
CARLOS	77

GIRLS
NAMES

	Success	Morality	Health	Warmth	Cheerful	Male - Female
ABBY	45	56	47	66	68	35
ABIGAIL	56	[103]	(22)	[76]	(24)	30
ACACIA	36	(24)	38	(26)	43	32
ADA	31	33	35	33	(29)	36
ADELAIDE	39	65	30	65	44	33
ADELE	41	[76]	38	[75]	40	(29) ♀
ADELINE	51	56	48	51	48	(24) ♀
ADELLE	55	52	39	55	55	32
ADINA	(27)	33	34	34	40	35
ADRIENNE	59	56	52	61	63	30
AGATHA	61	[73]	(16)	42	(2)	33
AGNES	34	[104]	(-1)	49	(4)	38
AIDA	(18)	45	(15)	38	(23)	40
AILEEN	[71]	52	60	61	45	(27) ♀
ALANNA	52	30	60	59	58	(15) ♀
ALBERTA	(24)	41	(29)	(25)	(26)	41
ALETHEA	41	47	44	49	48	36
ALEXANDRA	[77]	49	67	57	65	41
ALEXIS	[76]	47	[80]	58	51	33

KEY: Least - ○ Most - □ Feminine - ♀

The Name Game

	Success	Morality	Health	Warmth	Cheerful	Male - Female
ALFREDA	35	53	21	35	28	44
ALICE	22	78	40	92	70	28
ALICIA	59	52	60	57	53	20
ALISON	63	41	73	62	73	29
ALLEGRA	62	45	59	39	49	32
ALLIE	54	43	65	60	67	32
ALMA	27	69	33	69	37	39
ALTHEA	41	25	38	22	37	33
ALVA	16	57	21	22	19	38
ALYSSA	72	54	61	61	63	23
AMABEL	30	52	29	47	39	24
AMANDA	71	59	67	63	82	32
AMBER	42	19	71	89	88	27
AMELIA	51	101	31	86	28	29
AMY	52	59	65	92	73	25
ANASTASSIA	62	51	57	37	30	37
ANDREA	69	52	64	66	50	39
ANGELA	46	49	60	73	63	25
ANGELICA	65	54	61	58	53	15

KEY: Least - ○ Most - □ Feminine - ♀

The Name Game

	Success	Morality	Health	Warmth	Cheerful	Male - Female
ANGIE	50	48	54	55	69	30
ANITA	61	63	50	[85]	69	(21) ♀
ANN	[77]	[87]	[81]	[111]	[96]	33
ANNABEL	43	50	48	53	51	31
ANNAMARIA	60	67	58	[76]	54	(14) ♀
ANNELISE	58	62	58	[71]	61	(18) ♀
ANNETTE	62	60	60	63	62	31
ANTOINETTE	60	51	64	44	50	32
APRIL	37	36	66	[82]	[78]	(24) ♀
ARABELLA	(29)	40	35	35	45	31
ARACELLI	35	30	46	32	48	37
ARDELLE	46	47	38	36	41	(25) ♀
ARETHA	43	53	36	52	46	31
ARIEL	56	54	57	62	52	34
ARLENE	34	50	45	46	44	32
ARMEDA	(26)	34	30	(29)	(27)	40
ASHLEY	63	61	[81]	[71]	[78]	30
ASTRID	54	39	32	43	33	38
ATHENA	63	54	58	60	55	31

KEY: Least - ○ Most - □ Feminine - ♀

The Name Game

	Success	Morality	Health	Warmth	Cheerful	Male - Female
AUBREY	59	56	67	59	64	33
AUDREY	65	65	58	[73]	58	(27) ♀
AUGUSTA	52	65	43	53	35	38
AURORA	53	45	56	[78]	58	(24) ♀
AVA	67	38	56	43	41	(29) ♀
AVERY	46	49	58	51	49	48
AVIS	49	44	34	32	30	41
BARBARA	54	59	50	[78]	66	(29) ♀
BARBIE	(22)	(25)	[73]	59	[74]	(12) ♀
BEA	52	55	33	59	51	39
BEATRICE	40	[92]	(24)	[80]	49	34
BECKY	36	55	47	61	69	33
BELINDA	33	44	53	44	[71]	(26) ♀
BELLE	44	58	50	64	63	(20) ♀
BENITA	36	47	38	42	41	32
BERNADETTE	43	69	49	[82]	52	31
BERNICE	(26)	37	(22)	(23)	(20)	37
BERTHA	(14)	62	(-6)	63	35	44
BERYL	39	45	37	(25)	30	49

KEY: Least - ( ) Most - [ ] Feminine - ♀

The Name Game

	Success	Morality	Health	Warmth	Cheerful	Male - Female
BESS	39	48	49	49	45	33
BESSIE	35	63	37	58	56	(23)♀
BETH	43	[99]	54	[113]	[73]	(27)♀
BETHANY	57	60	57	67	56	30
BETSY	37	[71]	61	[88]	[74]	(26)♀
BETTY	31	59	37	54	47	30
BEULAH	33	49	30	45	43	31
BEVERLY	68	69	[75]	[75]	67	(24)♀
BEVIN	41	39	34	(15)	(28)	47
BIANCA	[70]	51	[83]	55	[73]	(23)♀
BIBI	(21)	(24)	42	47	62	(20)♀
BILLIE	45	39	53	42	50	46
BLAINE	67	49	65	49	52	51
BLAIR	[72]	41	[81]	45	60	39
BLANCHE	(29)	36	40	33	42	41
BLISS	(14)	(16)	37	(25)	52	33
BOBBIE	49	39	61	57	64	42
BONITA	35	46	46	61	51	(17)♀
BONNIE	(16)	41	52	63	70	(25)♀

KEY: Least - ( ) Most - [ ] Feminine - ♀

The Name Game

	Success	Morality	Health	Warmth	Cheerful	Male - Female
BRANDY	○29	○11	62	45	67	38
BRENDA	44	45	49	56	63	30
BRIDGET	34	○28	□81	61	□80	19 ♀
BRIGITTE	45	39	□79	61	68	24 ♀
BRITNEY	68	54	□76	62	63	31
BRITTANY	63	42	□89	□71	□94	21 ♀
BRONWYN	63	50	51	44	40	48
BROOKE	61	33	□104	□73	□74	25 ♀
BRUNHILDA	○-4	30	○-17	○2	○-23	50
BUNNY	○17	○23	58	57	□75	10 ♀
CAITLIN	61	50	□71	62	62	28 ♀
CALLIE	52	45	61	57	60	26 ♀
CAMILLE	55	□78	59	□76	42	25 ♀
CANDACE	65	36	63	54	58	33
CANDICE	61	48	□73	61	60	25 ♀
CANDY	○17	31	49	49	67	27 ♀
CAPRI	36	○26	□78	56	□86	28 ♀
CARA	50	38	61	43	55	30
CARINA	58	52	60	66	66	21 ♀

KEY: Least - ○ Most - □ Feminine - ♀

The Name Game

	Success	Morality	Health	Warmth	Cheerful	Male - Female
CARISSA	49	44	68	59	65	20 ♀
CARLA	52	61	54	67	63	30
CARLOTTA	47	44	51	47	47	22 ♀
CARLY	49	40	62	52	64	28 ♀
CARMEN	51	63	62	69	61	32
CAROL	60	69	62	[80]	61	24 ♀
CAROLINE	[70]	60	58	54	56	28 ♀
CARRIE	52	46	66	[72]	66	28 ♀
CARY	52	47	51	48	58	42
CASEY	52	56	70	56	63	44
CASSANDRA	67	(28)	[78]	58	70	18 ♀
CASSIE	49	46	67	65	[77]	21 ♀
CATHERINE	[75]	[92]	[72]	[85]	57	21 ♀
CECILIA	50	66	60	61	67	23 ♀
CELESTE	55	68	50	69	69	27 ♀
CELIA	48	53	47	42	44	32
CHANDRA	56	42	[74]	65	57	28 ♀
CHANTAL	57	51	68	65	60	29 ♀
CHARIS	49	42	48	31	50	32

KEY: Least - ○ Most - □ Feminine - ♀

	Success	Morality	Health	Warmth	Cheerful	Male - Female
CHARITY	28 ○	44	43	65	57	29 ♀
CHARLENE	42	45	57	53	66	30
CHARLOTTE	54	66	41	89 □	63	23 ♀
CHARMAINE	42	33	45	45	51	37
CHASTITY	37	51	64	68	56	19 ♀
CHELSEA	60	55	65	53	56	29 ♀
CHER	48	31	57	53	58	24 ♀
CHERIE	45	50	66	65	68	17 ♀
CHERRY	22 ○	25 ○	65	53	75 □	18 ♀
CHERYL	71 □	45	79 □	75 □	70	25 ♀
CHIQUITA	24 ○	22 ○	42	40	44	18 ♀
CHLOE	31	31	31	49	42	37
CHLORIS	32	38	35	40	33	33
CHRIS	63	60	76 □	54	59	49
CHRISSY	26 ○	40	53	52	78 □	27 ♀
CHRISTA	48	43	61	45	57	32
CHRISTINA	59	66	73 □	71 □	67	27 ♀
CHRISTINE	64	60	70	62	62	19 ♀
CHRISTY	53	40	68	70	83 □	27 ♀

KEY: Least - ○ Most - □ Feminine - ♀

The Name Game

	Success	Morality	Health	Warmth	Cheerful	Male - Female
CICELY	55	42	54	57	52	(28) ♀
CINDY	(27)	35	[89]	[76]	[97]	(24) ♀
CLAIRE	66	60	64	55	62	(28) ♀
CLARA	41	[89]	(23)	[86]	38	(28) ♀
CLARISSA	47	51	48	49	48	(28) ♀
CLAUDETTE	38	38	44	38	38	35
CLAUDIA	62	56	57	[71]	37	(26) ♀
CLEMENTINE	(26)	46	34	42	37	33
CLEO	50	52	40	58	46	37
COLLEEN	57	54	[72]	[82]	66	(22) ♀
COLLETTE	58	44	53	43	38	34
CONNIE	65	51	59	[86]	69	(22) ♀
CONSTANCE	49	[97]	39	65	(25)	(27) ♀
CONSUELA	(23)	50	(27)	41	(24)	33
CORA	31	45	35	42	32	37
CORDELIA	44	60	38	49	(29)	(20) ♀
COREY	49	44	68	57	68	44
CORINNE	57	54	59	55	52	(23) ♀
CORLISS	47	45	39	48	42	34

[On the page, values in ( ) are circled, values in [ ] are boxed, and ♀ is the feminine symbol.]

KEY: Least - ○ Most - □ Feminine - ♀

The Name Game

	Success	Morality	Health	Warmth	Cheerful	Male - Female
CORNELIA	58	[101]	(27)	63	(23)	34
CORY	38	47	53	36	54	42
COURTNEY	63	54	[77]	59	69	(26) ♀
CRISSY	30	39	[73]	56	[71]	(16) ♀
CRYSTAL	(27)	34	[80]	58	[71]	(19) ♀
CYBIL	61	42	61	31	45	36
CYNTHIA	55	42	70	66	[75]	(24) ♀
DAHLIA	50	43	50	55	50	(24) ♀
DAISY	(27)	48	58	[93]	[99]	(17) ♀
DALE	52	45	48	46	55	48
DANA	55	(23)	[73]	49	65	34
DANICA	60	50	59	56	57	(26) ♀
DANIELLE	[72]	42	[78]	55	66	36
DAPHNE	(26)	(12)	70	68	[97]	(23) ♀
DARA	35	34	33	(18)	31	42
DARBY	58	45	69	58	68	39
DARCY	55	48	56	59	69	30
DARLENE	(28)	(26)	[72]	58	[88]	(23) ♀
DAVITA	33	45	45	51	45	(24) ♀

KEY: Least - ( ) Most - [ ] Feminine - ♀

The Name Game

	Success	Morality	Health	Warmth	Cheerful	Male - Female
DAWN	34	38	64	78	69	22 ♀
DEANNA	57	49	59	62	50	28 ♀
DEANNE	50	45	68	55	69	34
DEBBIE	59	47	61	55	72	28 ♀
DEBORAH	67	55	72	66	67	21 ♀
DEE	31	35	52	46	54	34
DEEDEE	23	16	74	58	101	22 ♀
DEIRDRE	61	48	63	66	48	19 ♀
DELIA	68	59	51	76	63	25 ♀
DELILAH	29	43	35	35	35	31
DELPHINA	41	46	43	46	42	35
DENA	47	34	67	59	70	26 ♀
DENISE	49	35	77	54	83	30
DESIREE	46	32	60	36	59	30
DEVA	47	32	47	49	42	31
DEVINNE	42	30	39	44	42	27 ♀
DIANA	78	65	83	76	73	23 ♀
DIANE	57	59	53	55	59	30
DIDI	29	35	60	58	70	15 ♀

KEY: Least - ○ Most - □ Feminine - ♀

The Name Game

	Success	Morality	Health	Warmth	Cheerful	Male - Female
DIERDRE	58	38	57	45	65	31
DINAH	63	63	54	□ 75	□ 71	30
DIONNE	62	46	65	52	48	39
DIXIE	○ 18	○ 17	51	42	□ 72	32
DOLLY	○ 7	○ 29	36	39	62	♀ 25
DOLORES	○ 28	□ 78	32	63	36	♀ 29
DOMINIQUE	69	34	61	43	53	35
DONNA	63	48	□ 75	□ 78	63	33
DORA	50	63	37	62	54	♀ 28
DOREEN	45	59	56	□ 83	61	33
DORIA	49	48	38	49	43	♀ 24
DORINDA	35	31	37	○ 21	39	36
DORIS	36	65	40	□ 79	40	♀ 27
DOROTHY	50	□ 86	44	□ 85	□ 71	♀ 20
DORY	41	49	44	56	45	33
DOTTY	○ 11	○ 27	○ 27	48	54	30
DULCIE	○ 25	37	38	47	52	♀ 26
DUSTY	49	44	49	49	59	50
EARTHA	36	40	○ 27	35	30	38

KEY: Least - ○ Most - □ Feminine - ♀

	Success	Morality	Health	Warmth	Cheerful	Male - Female
EBONY	53	52	62	50	42	(28) ♀
EDIE	35	42	36	46	57	(28) ♀
EDITH	(8)	[90]	(16)	[86]	42	(28) ♀
EDNA	34	[78]	(10)	68	(28)	38
EDWINA	69	[96]	(16)	66	(25)	(28) ♀
EFFIE	(27)	54	40	56	48	31
EILEEN	59	56	52	61	66	(23) ♀
ELAINE	62	[76]	52	[83]	52	(27) ♀
ELEANOR	50	[85]	(17)	[81]	32	(27) ♀
ELISA	63	39	50	52	52	35
ELISE	69	54	66	[71]	56	(23) ♀
ELIZABETH	[76]	[86]	64	[73]	57	(22) ♀
ELKE	48	42	61	49	51	(28) ♀
ELLA	35	37	(27)	(27)	(28)	37
ELLEN	[72]	[93]	42	[85]	46	(24) ♀
ELLIE	52	52	65	64	62	(24) ♀
ELOISE	36	[96]	(24)	[85]	40	(28) ♀
ELSA	35	45	36	36	38	39
ELSIE	31	46	41	58	56	33

KEY: Least - ○ Most - □ Feminine - ♀

The Name Game

	Success	Morality	Health	Warmth	Cheerful	Male - Female
ELVIRA	(15)	(17)	(27)	(12)	38	39
ELYSIA	43	54	51	62	58	(22) ♀
EMILY	45	[101]	34	[93]	63	(22) ♀
EMMA	49	[103]	(26)	[102]	35	(22) ♀
ENDORA	(29)	31	(24)	(11)	(21)	38
ENID	(24)	48	(16)	31	(16)	(29) ♀
ERICA	63	34	[80]	63	[74]	(29) ♀
ERIN	64	45	69	65	69	39
ERMA	39	56	(26)	50	(29)	31
ERNESTINE	34	54	(24)	45	36	35
ESMERALDA	(25)	(28)	(17)	(16)	(28)	40
ESTELLE	43	68	37	65	(22)	(26) ♀
ESTHER	41	[104]	(23)	[78]	32	31
ETHEL	(25)	[93]	(7)	[86]	(23)	33
EUGENIA	(29)	52	32	43	33	33
EULA	(17)	39	(19)	(19)	(16)	39
EUNICE	(28)	37	35	39	(29)	36
EVA	54	67	46	70	44	36
EVANGELINE	39	38	33	40	38	38

KEY: Least - ○ Most - □ Feminine - ♀

The Name Game

	Success	Morality	Health	Warmth	Cheerful	Male - Female
EVE	49	65	43	[79]	32	(22) ♀
EVELYN	56	59	50	44	50	36
EVETTE	54	45	52	54	63	(23) ♀
FABIOLA	34	(27)	34	(22)	45	38
FAITH	34	59	48	62	40	30
FALLON	66	(28)	52	30	49	36
FANNY	(12)	[78]	(25)	[73]	59	(27) ♀
FARRAH	(22)	(5)	[89]	62	[82]	(23) ♀
FATIMA	36	43	40	51	35	(22) ♀
FAWN	(26)	(18)	49	36	38	33
FAY	52	49	50	[73]	70	(25) ♀
FELICIA	58	59	69	[86]	[78]	(19) ♀
FELICITY	(27)	38	41	37	55	36
FERN	(22)	51	39	68	48	35
FERNANDA	36	51	42	47	37	39
FIFI	(15)	(16)	50	43	54	(12) ♀
FIONNA	34	41	49	31	47	36
FLORA	(10)	40	31	33	(28)	35
FLORENCE	40	[79]	(17)	[95]	(29)	(27) ♀

KEY: Least - ○ Most - □ Feminine - ♀

The Name Game

	Success	Morality	Health	Warmth	Cheerful	Male - Female
FRAN	56	50	38	53	50	39
FRANCES	58	59	39	60	46	30
FRANCINE	54	54	48	63	56	(24) ♀
FRANCISCA	53	43	49	42	46	33
FRANCOISE	59	49	54	57	47	(28) ♀
FREDERICA	36	38	50	30	33	41
FREIDA	(23)	42	42	(22)	(26)	42
GABRIELLE	54	55	59	53	55	35
GAIL	36	34	38	51	48	32
GALINA	38	40	38	38	43	(27) ♀
GAY	44	41	40	54	51	(28) ♀
GENEVIEVE	41	61	38	65	36	(22) ♀
GEORGEANNE	42	54	43	64	58	(23) ♀
GEORGETTE	46	39	49	53	61	37
GEORGIA	42	52	51	54	49	34
GERALDINE	62	59	34	44	(23)	35
GERI	53	44	47	54	62	40
GERMAINE	45	55	48	42	34	40
GERTRUDE	(14)	[73]	(-5)	(25)	(-6)	41

KEY: Least - ○ Most - □ Feminine - ♀

The Name Game

	Success	Morality	Health	Warmth	Cheerful	Male - Female
GIA	36	29 ○	37	20 ○	31	39
GIGI	23 ○	23 ○	44	36	73 □	27 ○ ♀
GILDA	26 ○	40	38	31	37	39
GINA	35	34	62	39	66	34
GINGER	26 ○	21 ○	51	42	65	30
GINNY	45	54	55	64	63	21 ○ ♀
GISELLE	48	30	47	33	49	31
GLADYS	37	69	17 ○	68	42	31
GLENDA	42	49	51	55	41	20 ○ ♀
GLENNA	54	45	41	25 ○	40	35
GLORIA	64	72 □	54	81 □	53	27 ○ ♀
GLYNIS	35	30	28 ○	26 ○	28 ○	37
GOLDA	53	57	29 ○	57	40	25 ○ ♀
GOLDIE	27 ○	13 ○	56	56	87 □	31
GRACE	59	92 □	42	89 □	49	25 ○ ♀
GREER	58	44	42	43	43	47
GRETA	35	38	36	25 ○	36	35
GRETCHEN	41	55	58	61	59	30
GRISELDA	23 ○	75 □	14 ○	41	34	37

KEY: Least - ○ Most - □ Feminine - ♀

The Name Game

	Success	Morality	Health	Warmth	Cheerful	Male - Female
GUINEVERE	46	58	51	62	52	(19) ♀
GWEN	48	51	59	65	52	30
GWENDOLYN	43	52	49	38	44	31
HALLIE	47	57	63	68	66	(29) ♀
HANA	60	69	52	66	52	(29) ♀
HANNAH	67	[96]	51	[86]	55	30
HARMONY	38	55	65	66	48	(23) ♀
HARRIET	37	[75]	(9)	58	35	31
HATTIE	32	55	45	59	47	33
HAZEL	40	[82]	(25)	52	37	(29) ♀
HEATHER	50	33	[91]	[71]	[91]	(22) ♀
HEDDA	41	42	(29)	44	36	34
HEIDI	52	54	64	[79]	[87]	(24) ♀
HELEN	59	[78]	48	[76]	(29)	(22) ♀
HELGA	(27)	44	31	(9)	(11)	47
HELOISE	44	60	(29)	43	35	34
HENRIETTA	(27)	[96]	(8)	56	(20)	36
HESTER	34	66	(26)	55	(17)	41
HILARY	42	49	41	58	63	(25) ♀

KEY: Least - ( ) Most - [ ] Feminine - ♀

	Success	Morality	Health	Warmth	Cheerful	Male - Female
HILDA	30	39	(24)	(20)	(21)	38
HILDEGARDE	34	56	(27)	45	31	38
HOLLY	63	[76]	[76]	[98]	[101]	(23) ♀
HONEY	38	39	[71]	68	64	(17) ♀
HOPE	55	[104]	42	[107]	45	(26) ♀
HORTENSE	31	[75]	(3)	(27)	(6)	45
HYACINTH	38	50	41	47	40	(26) ♀
IDA	(25)	47	(29)	36	(25)	41
ILANA	46	42	59	53	56	(24) ♀
ILEANA	44	44	41	48	50	32
ILENE	47	49	46	59	51	(24) ♀
ILKA	37	44	53	46	45	(26) ♀
IMELDA	40	39	36	(16)	(9)	42
IMOGENE	36	60	(24)	50	35	36
INES	(23)	69	(29)	36	(14)	30
INGA	45	52	56	61	60	(26) ♀
INGRID	42	45	40	(22)	(23)	44
IOLA	38	53	36	49	48	31
IRENE	61	65	53	68	61	32

KEY: Least - ◯ Most - ☐ Feminine - ♀

The Name Game

	Success	Morality	Health	Warmth	Cheerful	Male - Female
IRINA	30	33	35	(23)	32	32
IRIS	40	53	44	37	44	34
IRMA	55	[76]	(14)	[72]	42	33
ISABEL	50	[87]	42	[86]	58	(29) ♀
ISADORA	38	50	43	44	42	(24) ♀
IVORY	50	48	48	55	49	(20) ♀
IVY	46	55	50	57	52	(27) ♀
JACKIE	58	31	[83]	66	[83]	34
JACQUELINE	[103]	55	[91]	[75]	70	(22) ♀
JADE	48	37	53	37	46	32
JANE	56	[78]	65	[72]	[75]	(27) ♀
JANET	56	48	[73]	[71]	[84]	(25) ♀
JANICE	57	50	66	59	57	(27) ♀
JANNA	54	54	55	54	48	(27) ♀
JASMINE	55	42	52	56	68	(29) ♀
JAYLENE	46	44	55	57	63	30
JEAN	65	63	50	56	45	45
JEANETTE	51	58	63	65	67	(24) ♀
JEANIE	48	47	57	62	62	(28) ♀

KEY: Least - ○ Most - □ Feminine - ♀

The Name Game

	Success	Morality	Health	Warmth	Cheerful	Male - Female
JENA	48	48	54	46	51	28 ♀
JENINE	53	52	53	60	67	28 ♀
JENNIFER	63	49	84	82	87	28 ♀
JENNY	68	65	79	81	86	21 ♀
JERI	45	31	43	55	58	40
JESSICA	79	40	93	85	83	22
JESSIE	46	40	62	50	50	41
JILL	63	52	83	55	81	30
JILLIAN	67	60	63	59	76	28 ♀
JINNY	47	56	60	75	72	25 ♀
JO	55	46	59	51	70	53
JOAN	75	56	52	52	33	35
JOANNA	58	52	58	59	60	20 ♀
JOANNE	67	60	55	51	62	30
JOCELYN	67	64	61	50	70	35
JODY	41	37	73	55	80	42
JOLENE	52	51	57	55	58	25 ♀
JOLIE	45	44	65	53	64	28 ♀
JORDANNA	63	59	58	52	51	30

KEY: Least - ○ Most - □ Feminine - ♀

The Name Game

	Success	Morality	Health	Warmth	Cheerful	Male - Female
JORY	46	33	50	40	57	44
JOSEPHINE	45	[85]	33	68	53	(28) ♀
JOSIE	47	46	48	53	53	36
JOY	48	57	53	58	67	(27) ♀
JOYCE	[76]	[79]	56	[75]	66	(28) ♀
JUANITA	(28)	38	32	34	35	31
JUDITH	[76]	[82]	51	[73]	37	(27) ♀
JUDY	52	47	64	61	[84]	(26) ♀
JULIA	68	[71]	64	[82]	65	(23) ♀
JULIANA	50	38	57	62	60	31
JULIE	[72]	68	[85]	[96]	[103]	30
JULIET	51	69	67	[100]	63	(17) ♀
JUNE	61	[87]	52	[100]	[81]	(26) ♀
JUSTINE	67	50	63	53	67	40
KALI	44	37	[75]	63	63	33
KARA	59	55	[74]	58	63	30
KAREN	70	[73]	[76]	[86]	67	(24) ♀
KATE	[75]	58	65	[82]	70	31
KATHERINE	[89]	[89]	63	[83]	63	(24) ♀

KEY: Least - ○ Most - □ Feminine - ♀

The Name Game

	Success	Morality	Health	Warmth	Cheerful	Male - Female
KATHLEEN	63	[78]	70	[89]	[93]	(21) ♀
KATHY	68	65	[84]	[76]	[84]	(25) ♀
KATIE	54	51	68	62	[79]	(14) ♀
KATRINA	64	52	63	68	[74]	30
KATY	54	57	62	65	70	(29) ♀
KAY	50	60	50	61	58	30
KAYLA	57	52	70	[72]	66	31
KELLY	56	45	[90]	65	[84]	(29) ♀
KENDRA	59	54	[71]	60	61	34
KIM	67	58	[93]	70	[88]	(21) ♀
KIMBERLY	[75]	64	[85]	[79]	[92]	(23) ♀
KIMURA	41	42	38	43	33	32
KIRBY	52	33	49	36	51	52
KIRSTEN	56	31	[92]	62	[73]	(26) ♀
KITTY	(29)	31	58	56	64	(18) ♀
KRISTIN	63	55	69	63	[76]	(29) ♀
LANA	50	(13)	[84]	54	[80]	(26) ♀
LANE	58	58	61	55	55	51
LANI	44	50	57	55	61	(22) ♀

KEY: Least - ○ Most - □ Feminine - ♀

The Name Game

	Success	Morality	Health	Warmth	Cheerful	Male - Female
LARISSA	47	37	67	54	65	○20 ♀
LATOYA	○29	30	41	42	60	32
LATRICE	41	38	48	49	49	33
LAURA	69	□71	□76	□76	□83	○25 ♀
LAUREL	□72	45	58	□71	54	○26 ♀
LAUREN	□80	66	□73	67	□72	35
LAVERNE	○21	58	39	64	65	39
LEAH	57	45	53	35	48	35
LEANDRA	52	47	50	63	52	○27 ♀
LEANNE	48	51	47	36	50	32
LEE	□74	51	63	52	63	50
LEIGH	68	54	60	55	59	○28 ♀
LEILA	54	44	46	55	54	33
LENA	62	49	53	□71	45	○27 ♀
LENNEA	46	41	49	45	48	33
LENORE	64	□89	35	55	38	42
LEONA	38	38	38	34	40	32
LEONORA	41	54	37	48	38	○22 ♀
LEONTINE	51	58	38	39	46	33

KEY: Least - ○ Most - □ Feminine - ♀

The Name Game

	Success	Morality	Health	Warmth	Cheerful	Male - Female
LESLIE	[74]	68	68	[71]	[78]	31
LETICIA	45	68	55	62	45	(26) ♀
LIBBY	(26)	45	(24)	59	53	31
LILA	37	44	44	44	50	34
LILIAN	38	[87]	44	[88]	49	(24) ♀
LILITH	47	48	35	38	34	(28) ♀
LILLY	32	46	40	40	40	30
LINA	48	48	45	55	54	(22) ♀
LINDA	[76]	58	70	[72]	49	(25) ♀
LINDSEY	69	62	[75]	[79]	[82]	33
LINETTE	44	49	53	49	55	31
LISA	64	41	[80]	56	[83]	(24) ♀
LISETTE	39	32	42	37	30	31
LIZ	56	47	49	41	67	35
LIZA	57	39	63	54	60	(21) ♀
LIZZY	(27)	(21)	37	41	54	33
LOIS	65	61	34	52	46	43
LOLA	(19)	(20)	38	45	35	36
LOLITA	(25)	33	51	41	49	(17) ♀

KEY: Least - ◯ Most - □ Feminine - ♀

The Name Game

	Success	Morality	Health	Warmth	Cheerful	Male - Female
LOLLY	(7)	(28)	(26)	44	54	31
LONI	44	41	48	40	60	38
LORELEI	49	54	58	62	61	(18) ♀
LORELLE	54	53	57	55	52	(28) ♀
LORENA	56	66	57	70	48	(25) ♀
LORETTA	63	66	54	[72]	55	(29) ♀
LORI	56	45	61	53	67	30
LORISSA	40	44	44	51	42	30
LORNA	63	37	70	41	55	(26) ♀
LORRAINE	58	69	66	[76]	61	32
LOTTIE	(29)	39	45	54	55	(27) ♀
LOUISE	45	66	34	[72]	49	36
LUCILLE	43	64	47	[71]	[78]	(26) ♀
LUCINDA	(29)	41	34	40	34	31
LUCRETIA	41	48	(28)	41	(29)	(24) ♀
LUCY	36	(27)	45	66	[88]	30
LUELLA	(24)	37	(26)	32	37	37
LULU	(23)	36	36	53	63	(20) ♀
LUPE	(12)	47	33	46	44	35

KEY: Least - ○ Most - □ Feminine - ♀

	Success	Morality	Health	Warmth	Cheerful	Male - Female
LYDA	40	44	42	43	40	○ 26 ♀
LYDIA	48	51	43	66	42	○ 29 ♀
LYNETTE	48	45	53	60	59	○ 17 ♀
LYNN	62	59	□ 71	□ 82	□ 82	35
LYNNET	46	47	49	○ 27	46	○ 29 ♀
MABEL	○ 28	□ 86	○ 17	□ 83	46	38
MADELINE	51	41	49	61	62	33
MADGE	35	49	○ 27	49	35	39
MAE	41	54	38	47	55	○ 29 ♀
MAGDA	36	○ 29	○ 25	○ 23	○ 26	42
MAGGIE	○ 26	63	36	□ 76	53	32
MALLORY	64	60	55	49	63	37
MANDY	○ 26	○ 10	□ 80	□ 78	□ 104	○ 29 ♀
MANUELA	○ 10	69	○ 19	□ 79	41	35
MARA	42	31	44	48	41	35
MARCELLA	59	35	41	39	40	33
MARCIA	66	60	69	□ 72	70	○ 23 ♀
MARCY	59	51	45	49	60	33
MARGARET	□ 78	□ 82	48	69	37	36

KEY: Least - ○ Most - □ Feminine - ♀

The Name Game

	Success	Morality	Health	Warmth	Cheerful	Male - Female
MARGERY	51	60	51	59	62	32
MARGO	64	62	69	[75]	54	44
MARGUERITE	55	54	40	54	48	(26) ♀
MARIA	34	[76]	54	[78]	46	(17) ♀
MARIE	59	69	51	64	66	(20) ♀
MARIETTA	55	54	44	57	50	(25) ♀
MARILYN	50	62	64	[79]	70	(21) ♀
MARINA	47	(25)	47	39	53	35
MARION	50	[80]	36	[78]	57	(23) ♀
MARIS	59	49	53	40	44	(29) ♀
MARISSA	58	40	48	66	54	33
MARJORIE	51	38	44	49	49	35
MARLENE	58	52	65	[72]	62	(26) ♀
MARLO	59	39	59	54	47	41
MARNIE	42	55	54	50	63	37
MARSHA	52	53	50	51	51	(24) ♀
MARTHA	47	[78]	33	[88]	36	33
MARTINA	61	43	45	33	31	45
MARY	[75]	[100]	65	[96]	65	(24) ♀

KEY: Least - ○ Most - □ Feminine - ♀

The Name Game

	Success	Morality	Health	Warmth	Cheerful	Male - Female
MARYANN	54	67	53	77 □	70	13 ○ ♀
MARYBETH	50	64	58	72 □	68	18 ○ ♀
MARYELLEN	35	69	47	76 □	52	17 ○ ♀
MARYJO	38	54	50	68	62	28 ○ ♀
MARYLOU	35	55	40	65	52	21 ○ ♀
MATILDA	17 ○	32	33	26 ○	25 ○	36
MAUDE	45	46	29 ○	37	31	43
MAUREEN	70	59	54	59	50	37
MAUVE	23 ○	38	29 ○	36	23 ○	30
MAVIS	34	34	32	30	34	43
MAXINE	63	28 ○	59	36	46	37
MAY	43	42	38	52	49	33
MEADE	50	42	43	33	41	47
MEG	57	66	50	60	55	30
MEGAN	69	51	78 □	62	59	33
MELANIE	38	48	74 □	83 □	93 □	23 ○ ♀
MELBA	30	47	32	46	32	32
MELINDA	59	44	65	76 □	78 □	28
MELISSA	56	49	65	69	67	25 ○ ♀

KEY: Least - ○ Most - □ Feminine - ♀

The Name Game

	Success	Morality	Health	Warmth	Cheerful	Male - Female
MELODY	38	53	61	63	67	(15) ♀
MELVINA	(22)	36	(25)	37	(27)	37
MERCEDES	62	37	47	(29)	42	42
MEREDITH	65	[71]	44	68	36	31
MERLE	48	45	49	54	48	49
MIA	43	43	46	41	51	31
MICHELLE	[71]	46	[75]	[86]	[88]	(28) ♀
MILDRED	35	[92]	(9)	69	(7)	44
MILLICENT	45	46	37	38	(27)	38
MILLIE	(24)	45	40	55	53	32
MIMI	(23)	(17)	34	40	62	30
MINA	43	40	46	44	47	(28) ♀
MINDY	41	37	56	53	[77]	30
MINERVA	(28)	33	31	(25)	(17)	40
MINNIE	(23)	51	43	62	70	(18) ♀
MIRA	44	39	41	50	43	(28) ♀
MIRABEL	(27)	60	(25)	57	50	(27) ♀
MIRANDA	52	62	40	65	48	(21) ♀
MIRIAM	49	60	38	49	41	(26) ♀

KEY: Least - ○ Most - □ Feminine - ♀

The Name Game

	Success	Morality	Health	Warmth	Cheerful	Male - Female
MISSY	37	45	72 (Most)	66	70	13 ♀
MISTY	53	48	71 (Most)	57	55	22 ♀
MITZI	37	41	61	70	75 (Most)	19 ♀
MOLLY	52	62	42	83 (Most)	66	31
MONA	35	28 (Least)	31	44	46	34
MONICA	51	42	64	61	55	28 ♀
MONIQUE	65	45	68	56	64	25 ♀
MORGANA	56	42	53	39	39	33
MURIEL	52	99 (Most)	17 (Least)	61	23 (Least)	34
MUSETTE	27 (Least)	19 (Least)	24 (Least)	23 (Least)	34	34
MYRA	49	82 (Most)	20 (Least)	44	35	37
MYRNA	35	56	30	44	39	28 ♀
MYRTLE	37	96 (Most)	5 (Least)	73 (Most)	5 (Least)	29 ♀
NADIA	57	54	61	63	54	35
NADINE	44	45	47	44	37	29 ♀
NAN	52	52	51	69	62	34
NANCY	70	66	59	61	59	26 ♀
NANNETTE	43	51	50	57	63	31
NAOMI	33	37	46	59	75 (Most)	32

KEY: Least - ○ Most - □ Feminine - ♀

The Name Game

	Success	Morality	Health	Warmth	Cheerful	Male - Female
NATALIE	61	48	[78]	[75]	[83]	(29) ♀
NATASHA	65	37	59	61	65	(23) ♀
NELL	43	52	44	62	55	(27) ♀
NELLIE	(26)	42	36	32	45	36
NERISSA	56	58	64	66	61	(27) ♀
NETTIE	36	53	37	54	47	(26) ♀
NICOLE	51	(28)	[78]	49	67	35
NIKKI	39	37	[71]	59	[72]	(29) ♀
NINA	42	58	63	[75]	[87]	(27) ♀
NOEL	43	48	50	54	50	43
NONA	46	54	43	47	37	31
NORA	47	[80]	37	[88]	59	31
NOREEN	51	50	42	50	59	(26) ♀
NORMA	44	[78]	(27)	59	(20)	40
OCTAVIA	42	45	39	44	34	(27) ♀
ODETTE	33	34	34	(20)	(27)	39
OLGA	(28)	[79]	(2)	42	(19)	56
OLIVE	(11)	31	(15)	30	32	37
OLIVIA	50	56	46	66	48	(25) ♀

KEY: Least - ○ Most - □ Feminine - ♀

The Name Game

	Success	Morality	Health	Warmth	Cheerful	Male - Female
OLYMPIA	[73]	56	60	59	43	30
OPAL	55	48	(27)	69	52	(28) ♀
OPHELIA	44	69	45	[82]	40	(23) ♀
PAGE	64	33	[82]	68	67	(23) ♀
PALOMA	54	48	57	52	53	32
PAMELA	[79]	63	64	[72]	62	(29) ♀
PANDORA	45	35	36	44	48	35
PAT	47	31	49	33	47	53
PATIENCE	58	[76]	40	64	49	(19) ♀
PATRICE	45	46	55	54	55	35
PATRICIA	[77]	[73]	66	66	61	36
PATSY	(29)	37	43	51	64	34
PATTY	33	39	54	47	[72]	34
PAULA	61	65	58	[78]	63	37
PAULETTE	49	53	54	63	55	(22) ♀
PAULINE	65	63	59	56	54	(27) ♀
PEARL	49	[82]	40	[90]	49	(28) ♀
PEG	(19)	39	44	39	47	37
PEGGY	(26)	49	42	42	54	31

KEY: Least - ◯ Most - ☐ Feminine - ♀

The Name Game

	Success	Morality	Health	Warmth	Cheerful	Male - Female
PENELOPE	31	56	51	[72]	62	(24) ♀
PENNY	34	50	50	48	51	(27) ♀
PHILOMENA	30	31	(23)	(29)	40	38
PHOEBE	43	38	65	55	55	(21) ♀
PHYLLIS	61	[75]	(22)	[73]	49	34
PIA	41	38	50	47	56	(24) ♀
PILAR	49	[71]	40	49	36	42
POLLY	30	[71]	52	[90]	83	(22) ♀
POLLYANNA	30	55	39	[71]	68	(18) ♀
PRISCILLA	(19)	54	56	58	59	(22) ♀
PRUDENCE	34	[115]	(0)	62	(-6)	(26) ♀
PRUNELLA	(27)	51	(8)	(9)	(-19)	37
RACHEL	67	47	[74]	[73]	[83]	(24) ♀
RAE	53	54	51	46	49	42
RAMONA	33	48	32	69	36	37
RANA	51	40	48	52	35	36
RANDI	39	34	70	60	65	41
RANITA	36	49	39	45	44	33
RAQUEL	69	36	[77]	57	[78]	31

KEY: Least - ◯ Most - ☐ Feminine - ♀

The Name Game

	Success	Morality	Health	Warmth	Cheerful	Male - Female
REBECCA	34	56	52	[83]	54	(29) ♀
REGINA	38	42	40	52	61	30
REMY	45	43	54	51	61	42
RENA	40	39	44	46	43	30
RENATA	50	50	41	53	40	35
RENE	52	45	56	46	48	32
RENEE	50	60	55	58	62	34
RHEA	[71]	55	64	58	50	(26) ♀
RHEANAN	40	(29)	37	(17)	(25)	40
RHODA	33	49	48	66	[82]	31
RHONDA	48	37	43	46	50	39
RITA	(29)	45	57	[71]	65	33
ROBERTA	(29)	[72]	31	62	45	36
ROBIN	64	44	[79]	[71]	[93]	34
ROCHELLE	33	33	51	39	54	30
ROLANDA	(26)	(22)	(26)	(23)	(27)	44
RONA	41	35	36	36	34	40
RONNETTE	(21)	(18)	31	(19)	33	48
ROSA	31	[89]	38	[88]	48	(29) ♀

KEY: Least - ◯ Most - ☐ Feminine - ♀

The Name Game

	Success	Morality	Health	Warmth	Cheerful	Male - Female
ROSALIE	44	42	59	53	63	31
ROSALIND	50	60	46	58	53	(23) ♀
ROSALINE	48	48	48	54	43	33
ROSANNE	34	52	50	[78]	66	(29) ♀
ROSE	(28)	[82]	36	[105]	54	(21) ♀
ROSEMARIE	48	59	46	59	47	(24) ♀
ROSEMARY	(20)	[92]	(22)	[90]	44	(21) ♀
ROWENA	49	55	42	54	45	30
ROXANNE	38	(-1)	[83]	54	[76]	(28) ♀
RUBY	43	44	43	62	42	31
RUTH	56	[82]	31	[73]	35	34
SABINA	42	43	55	52	49	(22) ♀
SABRINA	65	47	[82]	[81]	[80]	31
SADIE	(12)	(26)	52	[73]	63	33
SALLY	36	69	55	[75]	[73]	(20) ♀
SALOME	50	42	35	40	31	36
SAMANTHA	[83]	48	[96]	[76]	[91]	(28) ♀
SAMARA	55	50	51	56	54	31
SANDRA	63	52	66	69	65	(23) ♀

KEY: Least - ( ) Most - [ ] Feminine - ♀

	Success	Morality	Health	Warmth	Cheerful	Male - Female
SANDY	46	63	51	56	69	33
SAPPHIRE	43	30	55	41	51	(17) ♀
SARAH	61	[82]	57	[90]	49	(28) ♀
SARI	42	44	52	48	56	(29) ♀
SASHA	54	41	50	50	58	30
SCARLETT	38	31	63	52	48	(23) ♀
SELENA	63	49	50	51	49	(29) ♀
SELMA	(26)	47	32	38	(28)	36
SERAPHINA	35	47	46	48	45	(19) ♀
SERENA	58	49	49	68	45	(25) ♀
SHANA	48	44	66	54	57	33
SHANNON	53	52	61	50	63	33
SHARI	46	47	66	62	[72]	(19) ♀
SHARON	68	58	63	[85]	[86]	(26) ♀
SHEBA	36	34	49	40	35	(26) ♀
SHEENA	38	34	57	40	58	32
SHEILA	39	53	53	49	59	32
SHELBY	65	45	57	58	53	38
SHELLEY	54	48	[82]	59	[88]	(28) ♀

KEY: Least - ◯ Most - ☐ Feminine - ♀

The Name Game

	Success	Morality	Health	Warmth	Cheerful	Male - Female
SHERRY	50	35	[77]	58	[84]	(25) ♀
SHIRLEY	43	63	44	[81]	62	(21) ♀
SHOSHANA	37	57	40	44	52	(26) ♀
SIMONE	[71]	54	64	63	62	(26) ♀
SISSY	(5)	(28)	40	49	55	30
SOLANA	53	47	54	53	45	(24) ♀
SOLANGE	38	(27)	33	(19)	32	40
SONDRA	53	49	57	52	53	(24) ♀
SONIA	44	62	42	[71]	46	(28) ♀
SOPHIA	[74]	49	[71]	61	52	(27) ♀
SOPHIE	39	59	45	65	55	18
STACY	61	(28)	[90]	62	[105]	(22) ♀
STAR	46	39	52	49	62	(23) ♀
STELLA	43	[83]	33	51	35	32
STEPHANIE	57	33	[77]	[72]	[87]	(25) ♀
SUE	52	63	64	[98]	[87]	(26) ♀
SUMMER	35	38	56	56	[71]	31
SUSAN	[71]	54	[72]	56	67	(23) ♀
SUSANNA	59	57	61	60	57	(18) ♀

KEY: Least - ( ) Most - [ ] Feminine - ♀

The Name Game

	Success	Morality	Health	Warmth	Cheerful	Male - Female
SUSANNE	53	36	□72	57	63	○27 ♀
SUSIE	42	35	69	61	66	○13 ♀
SYBIL	52	60	41	48	36	40
SYLVIA	48	45	48	59	53	○24 ♀
TABITHA	31	○29	49	46	67	○27 ♀
TALLULAH	30	38	○28	47	46	31
TAMARA	54	53	60	52	55	○28 ♀
TAMMY	41	53	□74	□86	□78	32
TANYA	59	41	□93	66	□74	35
TARA	56	45	62	49	57	32
TASHA	54	48	61	57	53	35
TATIANA	53	48	55	45	54	31
TEMPEST	50	38	57	44	35	30
TERESA	61	□79	63	□75	66	33
TERRY	47	○23	□73	65	□79	44
TESS	34	50	43	67	57	36
TESSA	50	57	62	59	62	○29 ♀
THALIA	44	60	43	58	45	○26 ♀
THEA	43	51	40	47	37	33

KEY: Least - ○ Most - □ Feminine - ♀

	Success	Morality	Health	Warmth	Cheerful	Male - Female
THELMA	35	[99]	(23)	[88]	40	33
THEODORA	57	[101]	(25)	[72]	(24)	37
THERESA	56	60	57	58	59	(21) ♀
TIA	48	51	56	61	60	(27) ♀
TIFFANY	(26)	(12)	[88]	46	[88]	(24) ♀
TILLY	(13)	30	32	43	65	35
TINA	42	(27)	[77]	[72]	[79]	(23) ♀
TINE	43	44	49	50	54	34
TITANIA	54	45	49	41	34	33
TONI	60	55	64	50	[73]	48
TORY	59	43	61	45	58	48
TRACY	64	(20)	[93]	51	[87]	(28) ♀
TRICIA	63	48	58	48	55	33
TRINA	43	(29)	47	39	62	31
TRINITY	43	53	59	55	48	(24) ♀
TRIXIE	(3)	(-18)	53	(29)	[91]	(18) ♀
TRUDY	30	53	43	45	53	33
TUESDAY	43	44	69	53	68	33
URSULA	43	48	(24)	34	(-6)	32

KEY: Least - ◯ Most - ☐ Feminine - ♀

The Name Game

	Success	Morality	Health	Warmth	Cheerful	Male - Female
VALENTINA	40	44	48	54	46	(23) ♀
VALERIE	44	37	[82]	[73]	[87]	(25) ♀
VANESSA	65	42	[71]	[72]	[78]	(22) ♀
VELMA	32	35	(25)	50	38	37
VENUS	32	(16)	41	37	50	32
VERA	33	[85]	(26)	[83]	48	(29) ♀
VERNA	36	49	32	45	31	33
VERONICA	53	30	58	38	43	35
VICKI	54	39	61	52	63	(27) ♀
VICTORIA	[82]	[86]	64	[71]	50	(24) ♀
VILMA	39	53	31	35	(27)	(29) ♀
VIOLA	(25)	58	(29)	50	47	(26) ♀
VIOLET	31	60	38	[71]	54	(24) ♀
VIRGINIA	68	[80]	43	68	38	(22) ♀
VIVIAN	42	44	64	[72]	66	(25) ♀
WANDA	(21)	34	(27)	32	30	33
WENDY	65	42	64	[92]	[84]	(27) ♀
WENONAH	(20)	32	(19)	(15)	(22)	35
WESLEY	55	42	51	50	46	55

KEY: Least - ○ Most - □ Feminine - ♀

The Name Game

	Success	Morality	Health	Warmth	Cheerful	Male - Female
WHITNEY	64	48	□ 75	□ 75	□ 73	31
WILHELMINA	○ 25	30	30	○ 15	33	38
WILMA	○ 1	□ 75	○ 9	□ 79	○ 25	38
WINNIE	32	47	50	63	65	♀ 26
WINNIFRED	48	49	32	41	37	45
WYNN	42	40	32	39	46	46
XAVIERA	46	30	38	49	35	34
YASMIN	44	41	43	38	39	33
YOKO	34	30	30	36	35	43
YOLANDA	42	56	60	48	61	32
YVETTE	45	34	58	55	58	♀ 27
YVONNE	65	44	64	59	62	♀ 28
ZELDA	○ 29	□ 78	○ 7	34	○ 16	45
ZINA	45	40	32	38	39	♀ 28
ZOILA	○ 29	32	○ 25	○ 17	○ 21	42
ZSA ZSA	35	○ 19	59	38	52	♀ 11

KEY: Least - ○ Most - □ Feminine - ♀

Chapter Twelve

Female Names that Imply Success

The following female names are commonly associated with "success," which includes ambition, intelligence and creativity:

JACQUELINE	103	BLAIR	72
KATHERINE	89	DANIELLE	72
SAMANTHA	83	ELLEN	72
VICTORIA	82	JULIE	72
LAUREN	80	LAUREL	72
JESSICA	79	AILEEN	71
PAMELA	79	AMANDA	71
DIANA	78	CHERYL	71
MARGARET	78	MICHELLE	71
ALEXANDRA	77	RHEA	71
ANN	77	SIMONE	71
PATRICIA	77	SUSAN	71
ALEXIS	76	BIANCA	70
ELIZABETH	76	CAROLINE	70
JOYCE	76	KAREN	70
JUDITH	76	MAUREEN	70
LINDA	76	NANCY	70
CATHERINE	75	ANDREA	69
JOAN	75	DOMINIQUE	69
KATE	75	EDWINA	69
KIMBERLY	75	ELISE	69
MARY	75	LAURA	69
LEE	74	LINDSEY	69
LESLIE	74	MEGAN	69
SOPHIA	74	RAQUEL	69
OLYMPIA	73	BEVERLY	68
ALYSSA	72	BRITNEY	68

DELIA	68
JENNY	68
JULIA	68
KATHY	68
LEIGH	68
SHARON	68
VIRGINIA	68
AVA	67
BLAINE	67
CASSANDRA	67
DEBORAH	67
HANNAH	67
JILLIAN	67
JOANNE	67
JOCELYN	67
JUSTINE	67
KIM	67
RACHEL	67
CLAIRE	66
FALLON	66
MARCIA	66
ANGELICA	65
AUDREY	65
CANDACE	65
CONNIE	65
JEAN	65
LOIS	65
MEREDITH	65
MONIQUE	65
NATASHA	65
PAULINE	65
SABRINA	65
SHELBY	65
VANESSA	65
WENDY	65
YVONNE	65
CHRISTINE	64
ERIN	64
GLORIA	64
KATRINA	64
LENORE	64
LISA	64
MALLORY	64
MARGO	64
PAGE	64
ROBIN	64
TRACY	64
WHITNEY	64
ALISON	63
ASHLEY	63
ATHENA	63
BRITTANY	63
BRONWYN	63
CHRIS	63
COURTNEY	63
DINAH	63
DONNA	63
ELISA	63
ERICA	63
HOLLY	63
JENNIFER	63
JILL	63
JORDANNA	63
KATHLEEN	63
KRISTIN	63
LORETTA	63
LORNA	63
MAXINE	63
SANDRA	63
SELENA	63
TRICIA	63
ALLEGRA	62

Chapter Thirteen

Female Names that Suggest Morality

The following table includes female names with the highest connotations of morality:

PRUDENCE	115	KATHERINE	89
HOPE	104	LENORE	89
ESTHER	104	CLARA	89
AGNES	104	ROSA	89
ABIGAIL	103	ANN	87
EMMA	103	JUNE	87
CORNELIA	101	ISABEL	87
THEODORA	101	LILIAN	87
AMELIA	101	VICTORIA	86
EMILY	101	ELIZABETH	86
MARY	100	DOROTHY	86
MURIEL	99	MABEL	86
BETH	99	ELEANOR	85
THELMA	99	JOSEPHINE	85
CONSTANCE	97	VERA	85
EDWINA	96	STELLA	83
HANNAH	96	MARGARET	82
MYRTLE	96	JUDITH	82
ELOISE	96	SARAH	82
HENRIETTA	96	RUTH	82
ELLEN	93	MYRA	82
ETHEL	93	PEARL	82
CATHERINE	92	HAZEL	82
GRACE	92	ROSE	82
BEATRICE	92	VIRGINIA	80
MILDRED	92	MARION	80
ROSEMARY	92	NORA	80
EDITH	90	JOYCE	79

TERESA	79	POLLY	71
FLORENCE	79	BEVERLY	69
OLGA	79	CAROL	69
KATHLEEN	78	HANA	69
HELEN	78	MARIE	69
JANE	78	LORRAINE	69
CAMILLE	78	JULIET	69
MARTHA	78	OPHELIE	69
NORMA	78	BERNADETTE	69
EDNA	78	GLADYS	69
ZELDA	78	SALLY	69
DOLORES	78	MARYELLEN	69
ALICE	78	ALMA	69
FANNY	78	INES	69
HOLLY	76	MANUELA	69
ELAINE	76	LESLIE	68
PATIENCE	76	JULIE	68
IRMA	76	CELESTE	68
ADELE	76	LETICIA	68
MARIA	76	ESTELLE	68
PHYLLIS	75	ANNAMARIA	67
HARRIET	75	EVA	67
HORTENSE	75	MARYANN	67
GRISELDA	75	LAUREN	66
WILMA	75	NANCY	66
PATRICIA	73	LORETTA	66
KAREN	73	CHRISTINA	66
AGATHA	73	MEG	66
GERTRUDE	73	LORENA	66
GLORIA	72	CHARLOTTE	66
ROBERTA	72	CECILIA	66
LAURA	71	LOUISE	66
JULIA	71	HESTER	66
MEREDITH	71	DIANA	65
PILAR	71	JENNY	65
BETSY	71	KATHY	65

Chapter Fourteen

Female Names that Imply Health

The following female names are strongly associated with healthfulness:

BROOKE	104	PAGE	82
SAMANTHA	96	ANN	81
KIM	93	ASHLEY	81
TANYA	93	BLAIR	81
JESSICA	93	BRIDGET	81
TRACY	93	ALEXIS	80
KIRSTEN	92	LISA	80
JACQUELINE	91	ERICA	80
HEATHER	91	CRYSTAL	80
KELLY	90	MANDY	80
STACY	90	JENNY	79
BRITTANY	89	CHERYL	79
CINDY	89	ROBIN	79
FARRAH	89	BRIGITTE	79
TIFFANY	88	MEGAN	78
JULIE	85	NATALIE	78
KIMBERLY	85	DANIELLE	78
KATHY	84	CASSANDRA	78
JENNIFER	84	NICOLE	78
LANA	84	CAPRI	78
DIANA	83	COURTNEY	77
JILL	83	RAQUEL	77
BIANCA	83	SHERRY	77
JACKIE	83	DENISE	77
ROXANNE	83	STEPHANIE	77
SHELLEY	82	TINA	77
SABRINA	82	HOLLY	76
VALERIE	82	KAREN	76

LAURA	76
CHRIS	76
BRITNEY	76
BEVERLY	75
LINDSEY	75
WHITNEY	75
DONNA	75
MICHELLE	75
KALI	75
KARA	74
TAMMY	74
MELANIE	74
RACHEL	74
CHANDRA	74
DEEDEE	74
LAUREN	73
CHRISTINA	73
CANDICE	73
JANET	73
ALISON	73
CRISSY	73
JODY	73
BARBIE	73
DANA	73
TERRY	73
CATHERINE	72
DEBORAH	72
SUSAN	72
COLLEEN	72
MISSY	72
SUSANNE	72
DARLENE	72
LYNN	71
KENDRA	71
CAITLIN	71
SOPHIA	71
MISTY	71
VANESSA	71
HONEY	71
NIKKI	71
AMBER	71
KATHLEEN	70
CHRISTINE	70
LINDA	70
CASEY	70
KAYLA	70
CYNTHIA	70
LORNA	70
RANDI	70
DAPHNE	70
MARGO	69
MARCIA	69
FELICIA	69
KRISTIN	69
ERIN	69
DARBY	69
TUESDAY	69
SUSIE	69
LESLIE	68
CHANTAL	68
KATIE	68
MONIQUE	68
DEANNE	68
CARISSA	68
COREY	68
CHRISTY	68
JULIET	67
AMANDA	67
AUBREY	67
ALEXANDRA	67
CASSIE	67
LARISSA	67

Chapter Fifteen

Female Names that Imply Warmth

The following female names had the highest warmth ratings:

BETH	113	NORA	88
ANN	111	MARTHA	88
HOPE	107	THELMA	88
ROSE	105	KAREN	86
EMMA	102	MICHELLE	86
JULIET	100	TAMMY	86
JUNE	100	FELICIA	86
HOLLY	98	CONNIE	86
SUE	98	HANNAH	86
JULIE	96	ISABEL	86
MARY	96	AMELIA	86
FLORENCE	95	CLARA	86
DAISY	93	EDITH	86
EMILY	93	ETHEL	86
AMY	92	JESSICA	85
WENDY	92	CATHERINE	85
ALICE	92	SHARON	85
SARAH	90	ANITA	85
POLLY	90	DOROTHY	85
PEARL	90	ELLEN	85
ROSEMARY	90	ELOISE	85
AMBER	89	MELANIE	83
KATHLEEN	89	KATHERINE	83
GRACE	89	DOREEN	83
CHARLOTTE	89	ELAINE	83
BETSY	88	REBECCA	83
LILIAN	88	MOLLY	83
ROSA	88	VERA	83

MABEL	83
JENNIFER	82
COLLEEN	82
LYNN	82
APRIL	82
KATE	82
JULIA	82
BERNADETTE	82
OPHELIA	82
SABRINA	81
JENNY	81
GLORIA	81
SHIRLEY	81
ELEANOR	81
CAROL	80
BEATRICE	80
KIMBERLY	79
LINDSEY	79
MARILYN	79
HEIDI	79
EVE	79
DORIS	79
MANUELA	79
WILMA	79
MANDY	78
DONNA	78
DAWN	78
PAULA	78
AURORA	78
MARIA	78
BARBARA	78
ROSANNE	78
MARION	78
ESTHER	78
MARYANN	77
SAMANTHA	76
CINDY	76
KATHY	76
DIANA	76
LAURA	76
LORRAINE	76
MELINDA	76
CAMILLE	76
ANNAMARIA	76
DELIA	76
HELEN	76
MARYELLEN	76
MAGGIE	76
ABIGAIL	76
JACQUELINE	75
CHERYL	75
NATALIE	75
BEVERLY	75
WHITNEY	75
MARGO	75
TERESA	75
NINA	75
JINNY	75
JOYCE	75
SALLY	75
DINAH	75
ADELE	75
BROOKE	73
VALERIE	73
RACHEL	73
ELIZABETH	73
ANGELA	73
AUDREY	73
SADIE	73
JUDITH	73
FAY	73
RUTH	73

Chapter Sixteen

Female Names that Suggest Cheerfulness

Obviously women are more cheerful than men because their names rank higher:

STACY	105	HEIDI	87
MANDY	104	NINA	87
JULIE	103	VALERIE	87
HOLLY	101	STEPHANIE	87
DEEDEE	101	GOLDIE	87
DAISY	99	TRACY	87
CINDY	97	SHARON	86
DAPHNE	97	JENNY	86
ANN	96	CAPRI	86
BRITTANY	94	WENDY	84
KATHLEEN	93	KATHY	84
MELANIE	93	JANET	84
ROBIN	93	KELLY	84
KIMBERLY	92	JUDY	84
SAMANTHA	91	SHERRY	84
HEATHER	91	POLLY	83
TRIXIE	91	JESSICA	83
AMBER	88	LAURA	83
MICHELLE	88	NATALIE	83
KIM	88	RACHEL	83
LUCY	88	CHRISTY	83
SHELLEY	88	JACKIE	83
DARLENE	88	LISA	83
TIFFANY	88	DENISE	83
SUE	87	LYNN	82
JENNIFER	87	LINDSEY	82

RHODA	82
AMANDA	82
FARRAH	82
JUNE	81
JILL	81
SABRINA	80
BRIDGET	80
JODY	80
LANA	80
TINA	79
TERRY	79
KATIE	79
TAMMY	78
FELICIA	78
APRIL	78
MELINDA	78
VANESSA	78
ASHLEY	78
LESLIE	78
LUCILLE	78
RAQUEL	78
CHRISSY	78
CASSIE	77
MINDY	77
KRISTIN	76
JILLIAN	76
ROXANNE	76
JANE	75
MITZI	75
CYNTHIA	75
NAOMI	75
BUNNY	75
CHERRY	75
BETSY	74
BROOKE	74
KATRINA	74
TANYA	74
ERICA	74
BARBIE	74
BETH	73
AMY	73
DIANA	73
WHITNEY	73
SALLY	73
KIRSTEN	73
ALISON	73
BIANCA	73
TONI	73
GIGI	73
JINNY	72
LAUREN	72
SHARI	72
NIKKI	72
DEBBIE	72
PATTY	72
DIXIE	72
DOROTHY	71
DINAH	71
CRYSTAL	71
CRISSY	71
SUMMER	71
BELINDA	71
ALICE	70
KATE	70
MARILYN	70
MARYANN	70
JACQUELINE	70
CHERYL	70
FAY	70
MARCIA	70
MISSY	70
KATY	70

Chapter Seventeen

Female Names that Imply Femininity

In using the femininity ratings for female names, it is important for you to remember that these ratings have a range from 10 (for very high femininity) to around 60 (for very unfeminine names).

BUNNY	10	MINNIE	18
ZSA ZSA	11	CASSANDRA	18
BARBIE	12	MARYBETH	18
FIFI	12	POLLYANNA	18
MARYANN	13	KITTY	18
MISSY	13	ANNELISE	18
SUSIE	13	LORELEI	18
KATIE	14	SUSANNA	18
ANNAMARIA	14	SOPHIE	18
DIDI	15	CHIQUITA	18
MELODY	15	BRIDGET	19
ALANNA	15	FELICIA	19
ANGELICA	15	MITZI	19
CRISSY	16	SHARI	19
DAISY	17	CRYSTAL	19
CHERIE	17	CHRISTINE	19
HONEY	17	CHASTITY	19
JULIET	17	GUINEVERE	19
LYNETTE	17	PATIENCE	19
MARYELLEN	17	DEIRDRE	19
BONITA	17	SERAPHINA	19
SAPPHIRE	17	SALLY	20
LOLITA	17	DOROTHY	20
MARIA	17	MARIE	20
TRIXIE	18	CARISSA	20
CHERRY	18	LARISSA	20

BELLE	20	COLLEEN	22
LULU	20	EMILY	22
BIBI	20	LANI	22
JOANNA	20	PRISCILLA	22
ALICIA	20	ELYSIA	22
IVORY	20	ELIZABETH	22
GLENDA	20	PAULETTE	22
CORDELIA	20	MISTY	22
BRITTANY	21	LINA	22
KATHLEEN	21	SABINA	22
KIM	21	CARLOTTA	22
JENNY	21	VIRGINIA	22
CASSIE	21	LEONORA	22
MARILYN	21	GENEVIEVE	22
ANITA	21	EMMA	22
DEBORAH	21	FATIMA	22
CARINA	21	EVE	22
GINNY	21	HELEN	22
SHIRLEY	21	HOLLY	23
LIZA	21	DAPHNE	23
THERESA	21	MELANIE	23
CATHERINE	21	KIMBERLY	23
PHOEBE	21	DARLENE	23
ROSE	21	FARRAH	23
MARYLOU	21	TINA	23
MIRANDA	21	DIANA	23
ROSEMARY	21	BIANCA	23
STACY	22	MARCIA	23
DEEDEE	22	PAGE	23
HEATHER	22	CECILIA	23
POLLY	22	SUSAN	23
JESSICA	22	EILEEN	23
VANESSA	22	JULIA	23
JACQUELINE	22	SANDRA	23
CONNIE	22	NATASHA	23
DAWN	22	CHARLOTTE	23

Appendix

Background of the Approach to this Book

Most of us are unlikely to deliberately and knowingly select offensive names for our children or ourselves; in contrast, we try to pick names we like and assume others will as well. But, if we seek to make a good impression or positive impact with a name, what are some of the positive qualities we might desire? To answer this question, we first skipped ahead a step and individually asked each one of a large sample of adults to use single words and list positive characteristics they wished to see in their children.

The frequency with which various positive characteristics were mentioned was tabulated and the 38 most frequently mentioned qualities were selected for additional study. These 38 positive qualities are given below in alphabetical order.

adventurous	good-looking	patient
ambitious	healthy	playful
assertive	honest	polite
athletic	humorous	popular
caring	independent	religious
cheerful	intelligent	respectful
confident	kind	responsible
congenial	loving	sensitive
creative	loyal	sincere
curious	masculine	successful
feminine	moral	trustworthy
friendly	obedient	warm
generous	outgoing	

You probably can think of positive characteristics not included in the above list. Chances are, however, that any characteristic you think of will be related closely to one or more of the ones given above. Let us take "happy" for instance. This certainly is an important positive characteristic and is absent from our list. However, our list contains the following very closely related qualities: cheerful, playful, humorous.

Take another example, "thoughtful," missing from our list. Again, you will find qualities on our list such as caring, kind, generous, or warm which are related closely. In short, you should find that the above list of 38 qualities is quite comprehensive.

The grouping of positive connotations

Given this reasonably complete list of positive characteristics, we were able, then, to step back to the original issue–how first names imply more or less of each of these characteristics. A second large survey was conducted in which participants were presented with a single first name and told the sex for which it was intended. They were asked to imagine, for instance, a female person with the name "Laurie" and to indicate what that name alone implied about the person.

To report their reactions to each name, respondents had a list of the 38 characteristics and also were given a numerical scale so they could indicate how much of each characteristic was implied by the name. The scale ranged from zero (none of the characteristic) all the way to 8 (extremely high degree of the characteristic).

For example, a participant rating the female name Laurie might have judged that name to be low (2) on adventurous, moderate (5) on ambitious, low to moderate (3) on assertive, and so on.

Sets of 38 ratings, obtained for each of a large number of names, were then statistically analyzed to discover how the characteristics might be grouped. The statistical procedure, called *Factor Analysis*, showed us whether some of the characteristics tended to be associated (or correlated) with each other in the judgments of our respondents. For instance, did the qualities assertive and athletic go hand in hand? When people judged names as implying high assertiveness, did they also tend to judge the same names as implying high athletic quality?

Our statistical results showed that there was indeed a high level of interrelatedness among the various characteristics. Specifically, the following six distinct groups of qualities were identified. Below, each group is named after the most important or most representative quality incorporated within the group.

Successful: successful, ambitious, intelligent, creative

Moral: moral, obedient, respectful, religious, loyal, trustworthy

Healthy: healthy, popular, athletic, good-looking, confident, assertive

Warm: warm, loving, caring, kind, generous

Cheerful: cheerful, playful, curious, friendly, humorous

Masculine-feminine: masculine, feminine

Not all 38 characteristics are included in the above six groups. However, all 38 qualities are somehow implied by one or more of these six. It is also important to note that even though our emphasis was to identify and rate positive qualities implied by names, low scores assigned to names on these various qualities can be used also to ascertain the negative connotations of names.

Rating Names on the Six Basic Connotations

A third very large survey was conducted which resulted in the tables of name connotations given in this book. Respondents in this survey were given one name at a time and were requested to imagine a person having that name. They were then asked to tell us what the name alone implied about that individual.

To report the connotations for each name, respondents were given the six major groups of name connotations identified above (Successful, Moral, Healthy, Warm, Cheerful and Masculine vs. Feminine). They used a scale which ranged from zero (none of the characteristic) to 8 (extremely high degree of the characteristic) to rate a name with respect to each of the six basic connotations.

The following precautions were taken in obtaining ratings:

1. Respondents were told to think about each name and rate it as it was spelled and not to alter the name in any way while thinking about it.

2. They were asked not to rate their own names since we felt it would be difficult for respondents to be objective about their own names.

3. They were asked not to think about a specific person they knew with that name because we did not want them to think about the particular and non-representative characteristics of a single individual in judging a name. Instead, respondents were given a simple ploy to help them with the ratings. They were asked to imagine that they were about to meet a person for the first time (someone introduced by a friend, maybe a blind date, a new co-worker, or a new roommate) and that all they knew about this person was his or her first name. Given that all they knew was the name and the sex of that individual, how would they imagine the person and how would they describe that person using each of the six basic characteristics?

4. They were asked to be sure to keep the sex of the name in mind at all times.

5. They were told to read each group of characteristics carefully (for example, to remember that successful, ambitious, intelligent and creative were all grouped together under the first major characteristic **Successful**). They were requested to keep in mind the entire group of adjectives in each characteristic while assigning a single numerical value to a name for that characteristic.

6. In rating the Masculine-Feminine quality of a name, they were asked to assign high numerical scores for masculine names and to use low numerical scores for feminine-sounding names.

7. Finally, and most importantly, the respondents were cautioned to take their time, concentrate, and give as carefully measured answers as they possibly could.

Each of the names was rated by a total of at least 20 men and women. Average ratings were computed for each name. Ratings on a given characteristic (e.g., **Moral**) were transformed linearly to make them easier to understand. The linear transformation resulted in scales which had mean values of 50 and standard deviations of 20.

With these transformations, the various ratings average 50 and almost all ratings range from zero to 100. As a rating deviates upward from 50, it shows a higher level of the characteristic. Scores approaching 100 (or, for only a small fraction of the names, exceeding 100) show an extremely significant and high level of the characteristic. For most practical purposes, scores as high as 70 (one standard deviation above the mean) can be interpreted as implying a significantly high level of a particular characteristic and those exceeding 70 can be interpreted with even greater levels of certainty.

For scores below 50, once again those which are as low as 30 can be interpreted as implying a significantly low level of a particular characteristic. Those lower than 30 can be interpreted with even greater levels of certainty. Thus, scores as low as zero (or, for only a small fraction of the names, scores with negative values) show an extremely significant and low level of a characteristic.

An alternative interpretation of scores below 50 is to take them to mean the opposite of the positive characteristic–namely the corresponding negative characteristic: unsuccessful rather than successful, immoral rather than moral, unhealthy rather than healthy, cold rather than warm, and cheerless rather than cheerful.

It is important to keep in mind that for Masculine-Feminine scores, low scores simply imply femininity and the lower a score is, the more feminine is the corresponding name.

To summarize, then, our experimental work took us through three preparatory stages. In the first stage, we obtained a reasonably comprehensive list of positive personal characteristics. In the second stage, we grouped those characteristics statistically into the following six: Successful, Moral, Healthy, Warm, Cheerful and Masculine vs. Feminine. Evaluation of the last of these six, Masculine-Feminine, of course, depends on the sex of the child– femininity usually being valued for girls and masculinity for boys. Finally, in the third and most important stage, the data we obtained provided numerical estimates of the six basic connotations for each name in our survey.

About the Author

Albert Mehrabian came to psychology with B.S. and M.S. degrees in engineering from the Massachusetts Institute of Technology. He received his Ph.D. from Clark University and in 1964 commenced his academic career at the University of California, Los Angeles, where he currently is Professor of Psychology.

His research interests generally have centered on emotions. His numerous journal articles and books have dealt variously with the subtle ways in which emotions are communicated and influence social interaction. He has developed a comprehensive temperament-based approach to personality description and measurement. His work in environmental psychology focuses on emotional reactions to places and how such reactions determine socializing, work or preferences for various designs and architectural styles.

Recent applications of his theoretical work and measures have helped identify individual differences in characteristic patterns of eating and the emotional requisites to become a top-level athlete, or to function competently in high-stress situations. Other applications have produced a general system for naming products, services, corporate entities or persons in ways as to maximize preferences for the entities names.

Professor Mehrabian has served as a consulting editor to numerous professional journals, including the Journal of Psycholinguistic Research, where he currently is on the editorial board.